MEENA PATHAK'S
INDIAN
COOKING
FOR FAMILY AND FRIENDS

whitecap

I dedicate this book to my three children, Neeraj, Nayan and Anjali, who all share the same passion for food and love of spice as their mother.

First published in 2003 by
New Holland Publishers (UK) Ltd
London · Cape Town · Sydney · Auckland

Published in Canada in 2003 by Whitecap Books Ltd.
For more information, contact Whitecap Books, 351 Lynn Avenue,
North Vancouver, British Columbia, Canada, V7J 2C4

ISBN 1-55285-548-1

Senior Editor: Clare Sayer
Patak's Development Chef: Sunil Menon
Design: Roger Hammond
Photographer: John Freeman
Assistant photographer: Alex Dow
Stylist: Labeena Ishaque
Production: Hazel Kirkman
Editorial Direction: Rosemary Wilkinson

10 9 8 7 6 5 4 3 2 1

Reproduction by Pica Digital PTE Ltd, Singapore
Printed and bound by Times Offset (M) Sdn. Bhd., Malaysia

COOKERY NOTES
• Follow metric or imperial measurements but do not use a mixture of
  both as they are not interchangeable
• 1 teaspoon = 5 ml; 1 tablespoon = 15 ml
• All eggs are large unless otherwise stated
• Use granulated sugar unless otherwise stated

CONTENTS

Introduction 6

How we eat today 8
Preparing in advance 9
Using herbs and spices 10
Basic recipes 11

one **quick** fixes 16

two **everyday** family meals 30

three **easy** entertaining 54

four **home** comforts 76

five **special** occasions 100

Glossary of ingredients 122
Index 124
Useful addresses 126
Acknowledgments 127
The Patak's story 128

INTRODUCTION

The inspiration for this, my second cookbook, is really all about showing people how to cook good Indian food for themselves on an everyday basis. It is a recipe collection which reflects my life and how I like to cook and eat – I really wanted to prove that you do not have to attempt the whole Indian restaurant banquet experience in your home every time you want to cook Indian food. I lead a full and often very hectic life, however, I believe there should always be time for good delicious food – whether I am preparing a quick evening meal for myself and my husband Kirit, made with whatever ingredients I have in the fridge, a casual lunch for a friend or a dinner for a big family celebration. The demands of a busy lifestyle mean that I have had to adapt some classic Indian dishes to make them easier to prepare, however, I will never compromise on flavour. I personally do not enjoy bland food and want to show people that with a little bit of spice it is easy to produce the most mouth-watering dishes. It is important, though, not to confuse spice with heat – of course, some of my recipes do have a chili "kick" but what they have more than anything are delicious complex flavours which come from the spices I use. To me this is what real Indian food is all about.

Most of us (myself included) simply don't have the time to spend long hours in the kitchen and we also want to use ingredients that are readily available in the shops. "You are what you eat" is a statement that I strongly believe in so food should also be as naturally healthy as possible with an eye kept on the fat content. My love of spices is always at the heart of my cooking and I love experimenting with different flavours, using influences from other cuisines as well as from India.

All the ideas for the recipes have come from personal experience – the food I ate as a child in India, what I saw and experienced on my many travels and of course my family's favourite dishes. I sincerely hope you will enjoy cooking these dishes and will maybe also be inspired to create some of your own.

How we eat today

The way we cook and eat today has changed dramatically since I first came to live in England. As a child growing up in India I watched and learned how our food was prepared – ingredients were available only in season and everything was done as part of a ritual, from grinding whole spices to making fresh paneer cheese to filling endless triangles of pastry to make deliciously spicy samosas. I still insist on grinding my own spices but I recognize that, with more demands on our time, we want to spend less time in the kitchen and more time enjoying the food that we are preparing. Ten or so years ago, many of the ingredients that are essential to Indian cooking were hard to find, but now most of them are readily available in good supermarkets or Asian groceries. All of this is good news for Indian cooking.

One other reason is that people's tastes have become much more sophisticated – eating out is no longer reserved just for special occasions and as more and more people indulge in foreign holidays, they become more willing to experience different cultures and to try new flavours.

When my children were growing up we always ate together as a family at the end of the day and I still believe in the importance of family meals. However, there are times when you just need a quick snack or a simple bite to eat and so I have included some of my favourite "quick fix" dishes in this collection.

Menu planning

Traditionally Indians eat three meals a day but breakfast and lunch are often combined and snacking is practically second nature to Indians. A full Indian meal usually consists of a "wet" dish or curry, which could be meat, fish or paneer or legumes for vegetarians, one or two vegetable dishes, yogurt or raita, rice or breads and, of course, pickles. When planning a meal it is essential to create a balance and to have a combination of flavours and textures that complement each other. Colour is also vital – I always try to serve a green vegetable dish with meat and fish dishes. Many of the recipes in this book work particularly well with certain accompaniments and I have suggested these where relevant but don't be afraid to experiment with your own combinations.

Catering for large numbers

One of the most important things to remember when you are entertaining or cooking for large numbers is to make it easy on yourself. Cooking should be fun so if you are not an experienced cook, don't worry! Don't try to do something that is too complicated and choose some dishes that can be prepared ahead. A great way to cater for a large party is to let your guests help themselves – buffet food and snack dishes such as pappadums will keep guests happy and can look very impressive presented on large plates with simple garnishes and lots of pickles.

Preparing in advance

One of the things I have tried to do in this book is to make the recipes as easy to cook as possible. Many people still think that preparing and cooking Indian food requires a lot of preparation, but with a few time-saving tricks you will soon realize that cooking good, healthy Indian food is something that can be done at any time, for any occasion.

As you look through the recipes in this book you will see that some ingredients appear often and form the basis for many dishes. Garlic, ginger and onions are used extensively in Indian cooking. Buying and preparing these from scratch every time you want to cook an Indian dish can be time-consuming and laborious so here are some ideas and tips to help you on your way.

Garlic

A large number of Indian recipes call for minced garlic. One large clove will make about ½ teaspoon of minced garlic. You can prepare it in batches and keep it for later. Simply peel the garlic cloves and purée in a food processor or blender with a little water until you have a smooth pulp. This will keep in airtight containers in the refrigerator for up to ten days. You can also freeze minced garlic in ice cube trays kept specifically for this purpose. Once frozen, remove from the trays and store in the freezer in airtight containers.

Fresh ginger

Minced ginger is also a basic ingredient in many of my recipes. Simply peel the outer skin with a sharp knife and roughly chop the ginger into small pieces. Purée in a food processor or blender with a little water until you have a smooth consistency. Again, you can store this in the refrigerator in airtight containers or freeze as above. I usually leave my ginger unpeeled as there is a lot of flavour in the skin.

Onions

Onions are used in Indian cooking in many different ways – to flavour, colour, thicken or garnish dishes. If onions are being used to make a rich sauce for a meat dish they are usually fried slowly in oil or ghee. You can fry batches of sliced onions in advance and keep them in the refrigerator in airtight containers for up to two weeks.

Using herbs and spices

Herbs

The most commonly used fresh herb in Indian cooking is cilantro and there really is no substitute. Fresh cilantro can quickly lose its flavour but you can freeze it by washing the leaves well, leaving them to dry on a tea towel and then freezing in sealed plastic bags. It can then be used in cooking, although not as a garnish. Other fresh herbs such as fenugreek leaves and curry leaves can be stored in this way. Fried curry leaves are used as a garnish in dishes from southern India. You can prepare these in advance: simply fry in hot oil for 2–3 minutes. Remove from the pan with a slotted spoon, drain on absorbent paper towels and, when cool, store in an airtight container for up to ten days.

Spices

Spices are an important part of Indian culture – and not just because they are used extensively in the cooking. Many of the spices that we use today have been part of Ayurvedic medicine for thousands of years. Once you have discovered how spices work and what the most common flavour combinations are, you will soon be able to experiment and flavour your dishes to your own liking. See pages 122–123 for more information.

In Indian cooking there are spices that are always used at the beginning of a recipe, such as mustard seeds and cumin seeds. They are usually added to hot oil and when they start to crackle you add your "wet" ingredients, such as garlic, ginger and onions. Ground spices are added after you have added the vegetables – they need to go in last otherwise they will burn and change the colour and flavour of the dish. Garam masala is usually always added right at the end of a recipe – it only needs to be cooked for a few minutes but will enhance the flavour of a finished dish.

Spices only stay fresh for about four weeks. Ground spices deteriorate even more quickly than whole ones because their essential oils evaporate more quickly. It is always better to buy whole spices and then dry-roast and grind them, as and when you need them. The best way to store them is in airtight tins in a cupboard away from direct sunlight. Because I cook for my family every day, I grind up my spices in small quantities on a regular basis. Buy small quantities at a time and leave them quite coarsely ground – the finer they're ground the more quickly they lose their flavour.

Basic recipes

GARAM MASALA

There are countless different ways of preparing garam masala and in India, every household probably has its own special recipe, handed down through the generations. The basic mixture also varies throughout the regions of India. The mixture usually includes the spices cardamom, cloves, cinnamon and nutmeg. Here is my recipe for garam masala. This quantity lasts me for a few weeks – you may prefer to make less if you are not cooking Indian food on a daily basis.

150 g (5 oz) cumin seeds

60 g (2½ oz) coriander seeds

50 g (2 oz) green cardamom pods

35 g (1½ oz) black cardamom pods

20 x 2.5 cm (1 in) pieces of cinnamon
   stick

20 g (¾ oz) cloves

100 g (4 oz) fennel seeds

15 g (½ oz) bay leaves

2 whole nutmegs

Dry-roast all the spices by putting them in a preheated cast-iron frying pan. Stir over a medium heat for 3 minutes or until the mixture starts smoking slightly. Remove from the heat and allow to cool on paper towels. Transfer to a coffee or spice grinder and process until you have a fine powder (although I prefer to leave my mixture quite coarse). Store in a dry airtight container with a tight-fitting lid and keep out of direct sunlight. Use within one month.

CHAPATTI

Chapattis are eaten all over India as an accompaniment to most meals – they really are a national bread. The art is in the shaping – a good chapatti should be perfectly round and flat.

makes ten

225 g (8 oz) wholewheat flour, sifted

½ teaspoon salt (optional)

1 tablespoon vegetable oil

melted ghee or butter

Mix the flour, salt and 150 ml (³⁄₄ cup) water in a bowl. Add the oil and knead to a soft dough. Leave covered with a wet cloth for 30 minutes.

Knead the dough again for about 10 minutes then divide into 10 pieces using a little flour to shape them into round balls. Press out each piece on a floured board using your fingers. Roll out with a rolling pin into thin pancakes about 10–12 cm (4–5 in) in diameter.

Heat a flat frying pan or hot griddle. Cook each chapatti over a medium heat for 30 seconds and when one side dries up and tiny bubbles begin to appear, turn over and cook until brown spots appear on the under surface. Press the sides down gently with a clean tea towel.

Remove from the griddle with a pair of tongs and place directly over the heat/flame until it puffs up. Smear one side with a little ghee or butter and serve immediately.

PARATHA

Parathas originated in the north of India, where wheat is a staple.

makes six

225 g (8 oz) wholewheat flour, sifted
½ teaspoon salt
1 tablespoon vegetable oil
75 g (3 oz) ghee or butter, melted
extra flour for dusting

Put the flour, salt and 150 ml (³/₄ cup) water in a bowl and knead to a soft dough. Mix in the oil and set aside, covered, for 30 minutes.

Divide the dough into 6 equal parts and shape into round balls. Flatten and roll out into flat discs about 12 cm (5 in) in diameter.

Smear a little ghee onto the top of the paratha and fold it over into a semicircle. Smear more ghee over the upper surface and fold it again to form a triangle shape. Place on a floured board and roll into a thin triangle ensuring that the edges are not thick.

Place on a hot griddle. Cook for 1 minute then turn over. When the paratha begins to colour, brush a little ghee on one side. Turn over and cook. Brush a little ghee on this side also.

Cook for a few more seconds until the paratha is golden brown on both sides.

PERFECT BASMATI RICE

Rice is one of the main staples of Indian food, particularly in the south, where you are likely to eat rice at every meal. I always recommend using basmati rice as its aromatic flavour is far superior

to other varieties. Cooking perfect rice is really very simple.

serves four

2 cups basmati rice

4 cups water

Wash the basmati rice in several changes of warm water and then set aside for 20 minutes in a colander. Place the rice in a large pan and cover with four cups of hot water. Bring to the boil, stir gently and then cover. Leave to simmer for 10 minutes until all the water has been absorbed.

CUMIN RICE

This is a wonderfully simple rice dish that would be eaten every day in most Indian households – it is also very simple to make. I certainly prefer it to plain rice. The cumin seeds complement the fragrant basmati rice perfectly.

serves four

1½ cups basmati rice

1½ tablespoons vegetable oil

2 cloves

2 cardamom pods

1 bay leaf

1 teaspoon cumin seeds

½ teaspoon salt

Wash the rice in several changes of water and then leave to soak in a large bowl of cold water.

In a karhai, wok or large pan

Left: **Perfect basmati rice**

heat the oil and add the cloves, cardamom pods, bay leaf and cumin seeds. When the cumin seeds begin to crackle drain the rice and add to the pan.

Fry over a gentle heat until the oil coats the rice grains.

Add the salt and pour in 600 ml (3 cups) hot water, stir lightly to ensure that the rice does not stick to the base of the pan. Bring to the boil and then reduce the heat and simmer, covered, for 10 minutes until the water has been absorbed and the rice is cooked.

If the rice is cooked and the water is not completely absorbed, remove the lid to allow the water to evaporate. Remove the cardamom pods before serving.

CILANTRO AND MINT RAITA

This lovely bright green raita is delicious as a dip for pappadums, koftas or other fried snacks. It is also wonderful with kebabs. In an Indian household it would be made fresh every day but you can keep it for up to a week in the refrigerator.

serves four

150 g (5 oz) fresh cilantro

50 g (2 oz) fresh mint

1 green chili, chopped

4 cloves garlic, crushed

juice of ½ lime

250 g (9 oz) thick plain yogurt

½ teaspoon sugar

salt, to taste

Place the fresh cilantro, fresh mint, green chili and garlic in a food processor or blender and process to a fine paste. Add the lime juice and a little water if required.

Place the yogurt in a bowl and whisk in the green paste. Add the sugar and salt.

You can prepare this ahead by freezing the green paste without the yogurt.

MIXED VEGETABLE RAITA

This fresh tasting raita is a classic accompaniment to biryani dishes.

serves four

300 g (11 oz) plain yogurt

1½ teaspoons sugar

salt, to taste

1 teaspoon cumin seeds, roasted and
      ground (see page 22)

1 small onion, chopped

2 tomatoes, finely diced

½ cucumber, seeded and chopped

1 tablespoon chopped fresh cilantro

Mix the yogurt and sugar together with a whisk. Stir in salt and the ground roasted cumin.

Add the onions, tomatoes and cucumber and serve garnished with chopped cilantro.

DATE AND LIME CHUTNEY

One of my favourite relishes to serve with a hot meal, this also tastes equally good as a sandwich spread. It is unlike a fresh relish because it takes about 2 weeks to mature. Once opened, it will keep for about 2-3 months in the fridge.

makes about 2 kg (4 lb)

10–12 limes, each cut into 4 wedges

3 tablespoons sea salt

20 dried red chilies

1 tablespoon black mustard seeds

300 ml (1¼ cups) white vinegar

15 cloves garlic, peeled

1½ tablespoons minced ginger

350 g (12 oz) sugar

400 g (14 oz) pitted dates

225 g (8 oz) sultanas or other raisins

50 g (2 oz) crystallized ginger

50 g (2 oz) candied peel

The first step is to rub the lime wedges with the sea salt and place them in a glass or ceramic jar with a non-metallic lid. Seal the jar and leave the limes to mature at room temperature, or in the sun, for 2 weeks.

After 2 weeks continue with the recipe. Place the red chilies and mustard seeds in the vinegar and leave to infuse for 4–6 hours. Grind the vinegar and spices to a paste in a blender with the garlic and minced ginger.

Heat a cast-iron (not aluminum) pan and add the blended paste together with the sugar. Bring to the boil then add the dates, sultanas, crystallized ginger, candied peel and salted limes. Bring the mixture to a simmer, stirring constantly. Cook for 15 minutes. Turn off the heat. Put the chutney into sterilized jars while still hot and leave to cool.

Place a circle of waxed paper, waxed side down, over the chutney. Seal the jars and store in a cool place. Once opened, keep in the fridge.

Tip Sterilize jam jars and their lids (plastic-coated lids are necessary as the vinegar in chutney can corrode metal) by washing them in warm, soapy water. Rinse

thoroughly in warm water and dry well with a tea towel. Stand them on a baking tray and place in a warm oven (180°C/350°F/Gas Mark 4) for 10 minutes – this also prevents them from cracking when filling them with the hot chutney.

SPICED PINEAPPLE RELISH

This spicy sweet-and-sour combination is fairly common in India, served as an accompaniment with spicy dishes.

serves four

1 medium fresh pineapple, diced

1 small onion, finely diced (optional)

1 teaspoon salt

1 teaspoon ground cumin

1 teaspoon garam masala

1 green chili, finely diced

1 teaspoon sugar

1 teaspoon chopped mint leaves

Combine all the ingredients in a bowl. The onion is optional but I like to include it as it adds a bit of crunch. Toss gently with a wooden spoon, then serve at room temperature.

SPICED GRAVY

Gravy granules are not available in India as so many dishes are prepared with their own delicious sauce. For my children, however, I have adapted this recipe to be used with gravy granules. Serve the gravy hot with roast meats and mashed potatoes.

serves four

1 tablespoon vegetable oil

2.5 cm (1 in) piece of cinnamon stick

4 cloves

2 bay leaves

1 onion, diced

2 tablespoons gravy granules

500 ml (17 fl oz) warm water

1 tablespoon all-purpose flour

200 g (7 oz) canned chopped tomatoes

2 tablespoons mango or chili pickle

Heat the oil in a frying pan. Add the cinnamon stick, cloves and bay leaves and stir briefly. Add the diced onion and cook until translucent. Meanwhile, stir the gravy granules with the warm water in a mixing bowl or jug.

Add the all-purpose flour to the onion mixture and stir constantly for 2-3 minutes, making sure that it does not go lumpy. Add the canned chopped tomatoes and cook for 1 further minute before adding the gravy granules mixture. Keep stirring to avoid sticking and lumps. When the gravy starts to thicken stir in the mango or chili pickle then serve.

LASSI

Drinking lassi is a great way to beat the heat of the scorching sun in summer. Yogurt has many health-giving properties and this drink is perfect for settling the stomach – particularly after a very spicy Indian meal. It can be served sweet or salted.

serves four

400 g (14 oz) plain yogurt

75 g (3 oz) sugar or 1½ teaspoons salt

1 teaspoon roasted coriander seeds, crushed

pistachio slivers, to garnish

Pour the yogurt into a bowl, add the sugar or salt and 200 ml (7 fl oz) chilled water. Whisk well until all the sugar or salt has dissolved and all the lumps of yogurt are broken down, leaving a smooth flowing liquid. Stir in the coriander seeds and serve chilled, garnished with pistachio slivers.

ICED LIME WATER

This refreshing drink is served all over India during the summer. It is often served as a welcome drink.

serves four

75 g (3 oz) sugar

juice of 1 lime

½ teaspoon salt

fresh mint and lemon slices, to garnish

Mix 750 ml (3¼ cups) water and the sugar together in a bowl until the sugar has dissolved. Add the lime juice and salt and stir well. Serve with ice, fresh mint leaves and lemon slices.

Tip Squeezing fresh limes can be hard work. I put mine in the microwave for 10 seconds before squeezing them – this makes it much easier.

quick fixes

There are times when putting together a full Indian meal simply isn't possible and there are plenty of days when all I want is a fast bite to eat. This chapter is all about fast and delicious ways to eat when time is short – perhaps when a friend has dropped by for lunch or when you just fancy a tasty snack to keep you going. The spicy French toast is a great breakfast or brunch dish and takes just minutes to prepare, while my Bombay mixed vegetable sandwich is an interesting take on a classic snack.

EGGPLANT DIP

675 g (1½ lb) eggplants

2 cloves garlic, finely chopped

1 tablespoon finely chopped fresh
  cilantro

1–2 finely chopped chilies

1 tomato, finely chopped

¾ teaspoon salt

1 small onion, finely chopped

1 tablespoon finely chopped chives

1 teaspoon ground cumin

2 teaspoons lemon juice or plain yogurt

1 tablespoon vegetable oil

1 teaspoon garam masala

½ teaspoon sugar

hot naan bread, toast, pappadums or
  crackers, to serve

Eggplants are a wonderfully versatile vegetable – this dip is a particular favourite with my family and friends. It is great with pappadums but any kind of crispy snack will do.

Place the whole eggplants under a preheated broiler and cook for 15–20 minutes until the skin is blackened and burnt on all sides and the flesh is soft and "pulpy". Remove from the broiler and leave to cool to room temperature, before peeling off all the skin and removing the stalks. Place the eggplant flesh in a bowl and mash further using a potato masher or a wooden spoon.

Add all the remaining ingredients to the eggplant purée and stir well. Serve cold with hot naan bread, toast, pappadums or crackers.

Tip To cook the eggplants without having to watch them, wrap them in foil, put them on a baking tray and bake in a preheated oven, 180°C (350°F), Gas 4, for 20–25 minutes.

SPICY FRENCH TOAST

serves four

3 eggs

1 tablespoon milk

pinch of salt

½ teaspoon ground turmeric

½ teaspoon ground cumin

1 green chili, finely chopped

1 teaspoon chopped fresh cilantro

1 tablespoon melted butter

1 onion, finely diced

1 tablespoon oil

4 slices of bread, crusts removed

This recipe originally started off as a spicy omelette until I decided to dip bread in the mixture.

Break the eggs into a bowl and add the milk, salt, ground turmeric, ground cumin, chili, fresh cilantro, melted butter and onion. Whisk well.

Heat the oil in a pan. Dip each slice of bread, one at a time, into the egg mixture, ensuring that the egg coats the bread evenly. Transfer the bread slices to the pan and cook for about 3 minutes over a medium heat until light brown in colour. Turn the bread over and cook the other side for the same length of time. Serve hot.

Opposite: **Spicy French toast**

SPICED GROUND LAMB BALLS

serves four

500 g (1¼ lb) ground lamb or beef

1 egg

2 onions, finely chopped

1 tablespoon finely chopped fresh
   cilantro, plus extra to garnish

½ teaspoon ground turmeric

1 teaspoon chili powder

1 teaspoon garam masala

½ teaspoon minced garlic

1 teaspoon minced ginger

pinch of ground nutmeg (optional)

½ teaspoon salt

vegetable oil, for shallow frying

Cilantro and Mint Raita, to serve

These are usually served as a snack with Cilantro and Mint Raita (see page 13), however I always make double the quantity and freeze half so that I can enjoy them another time.

Combine all the ingredients except the oil in a bowl, mixing well, to make a fairly sticky mixture. Divide into 20–25 balls.

Heat the vegetable oil in a shallow frying pan. Cook 6 meatballs at a time, immersing them in the oil and gently swirling the oil around, to brown them on all sides, for 3–4 minutes. Drain on absorbent paper towels.

Sprinkle with cilantro and serve hot or cold with Cilantro and Mint Raita.

PASTA WITH **CURRY** SAUCE

serves four

15 g (½ oz) butter

½ teaspoon cumin seeds

1 large onion, sliced

1 teaspoon minced garlic

½ teaspoon ground turmeric

1 teaspoon garam masala

1 green bell pepper, seeded and sliced

1 red bell pepper, seeded and sliced

3 tablespoons light cream

salt

300 g (11 oz) cooked pasta, such as penne
   or fusilli

100 g (4 oz) grated cheese, to serve

My children love this recipe. They used to eat only plain pasta until they saw me changing the flavour of leftover pasta and now they will not have it any other way! Grated mature Cheddar tastes better than Parmesan cheese as a topping.

Heat the butter in a pan and add the cumin seeds. When they begin to crackle, add the sliced onions and fry for 5–8 minutes. Add the garlic pulp, ground turmeric and garam masala and continue to fry over a low heat.

Add the green and red bell peppers and cook for another 3–5 minutes. Add the light cream and salt to taste.

Add the cooked pasta to the sauce, sprinkle with grated cheese and serve hot.

SPICED **BEANS**
ON NAAN BREAD

serves two

1 teaspoon vegetable oil

1 teaspoon cumin seeds

1 green chili, seeded and chopped

pinch of asafetida

400 g (14 oz) can baked beans

2 mini naan breads

1 tablespoon cheese, grated

1 teaspoon chopped fresh cilantro

1 tablespoon chopped onions

This very simple dish is quick to make and is an all-time favourite with my husband.

Heat the oil, then add the cumin seeds. When they begin to crackle, add the green chili and asafetida. After 30 seconds add the baked beans. Give the mixture a good stir, then reduce the heat.

Place the naan breads on a baking tray. When the beans are heated through tip them onto each naan bread. Sprinkle the grated cheese, cilantro and onions over the beans.

Place under a preheated broiler and cook briefly until the cheese starts to melt and brown. Serve at once and eat hot.

MASALA PAPPADUMS

serves two

1 onion, chopped

2 potatoes, peeled, boiled and chopped

1 large tomato, chopped

2 tablespoons chopped fresh cilantro

1–2 green chilies, chopped and seeded or
 ½ teaspoon chili powder

¼ teaspoon salt

1 teaspoon cracked black pepper

1 teaspoon roasted cumin seeds, crushed
 (see Tip)

1 tablespoon lemon juice

4 ready-cooked pappadums

Pappadums are an extremely popular snack throughout India as well as in the many Indian restaurants outside India. My family loves this fun way of eating them, which they like to call "Go Crackers"!

Mix all the ingredients except the pappadums together in a bowl and divide into 4 portions. Sprinkle each portion over each pappadum and serve immediately so they don't go soggy.

Tip To roast cumin seeds, place them in a glass bowl or on a plate and cook in the microwave on high for 30–40 seconds. Crush coarsely using a mortar and pestle. Roasted cumin can be stored in an airtight container at room temperature for about 2–3 months.

CHEESE-STUFFED PEPPERS

serves two to four

150 g (5 oz) cheese, grated

1 onion, diced

1 tomato, chopped

1 green or red chili, chopped

½ teaspoon ground black pepper

1 tablespoon chopped fresh cilantro or
 fresh basil

½ teaspoon dried mixed herbs

1 teaspoon vegetable or olive oil

2 large red or green bell peppers, halved
 lengthways and seeded

Serve these peppers as an accompaniment to vegetarian or non-vegetarian main dishes, or as a snack with a green salad. An alternative, equally good version of the recipe below is to use 250 g (9 oz) of leftover mashed potato instead of cheese to fill the peppers, finishing off with a topping of grated cheese.

Preheat the oven to 180°C (350°F), Gas 4.
 Place all the ingredients except the oil and the bell peppers in a bowl and mix well.
 Rub the oil over the skin of the bell pepper halves and stuff them equally with the cheese mixture. Arrange on a baking tray, place in the preheated oven and cook for 20 minutes. Serve at once.

Opposite: **Masala pappadums**

BOMBAY MIXED VEGETABLE SANDWICH

serves two

FOR THE SANDWICH

4 slices of good white bread

15 g (½ oz) butter

1 potato, boiled, peeled and sliced into
   rounds

2 tomatoes, sliced

1 small onion, sliced into rings

10 slices of cucumber

salt and pepper, to taste

FOR THE CILANTRO CHUTNEY

150 g (5 oz) chopped fresh cilantro

2 tablespoons mint leaves, chopped

3 cloves garlic, peeled

2.5 cm (1 in) piece of fresh ginger,
   unpeeled and washed

¼ teaspoon salt

1 teaspoon sugar

2 green chilies

2 tablespoons lemon juice

This recipe brings back fond memories of my school days in Mumbai. I could never wait for the 11 o'clock break when we used to buy these sandwiches from the hawker stall outside the school gates! It is a great snack to take on picnics and is ideal served with hot soup. Once made, the cilantro chutney can be kept in the fridge for up to 10 days.

To make the cilantro chutney, place all the ingredients in a blender. Blend to a smooth paste, adding a little water if necessary to ease the blending. The resulting chutney will be fairly thick.

Spread the 4 slices of bread with the butter, then spread each slice with 1 tablespoon cilantro chutney. Lay 2 slices of the bread, chutney side up, on a work surface. Top with sliced potato, tomatoes, onion and cucumber, sprinkling salt and pepper between each layer. Top with the remaining slices of bread. Cut diagonally and serve.

SPICED FRIED FISH

serves two

½ teaspoon minced ginger

½ teaspoon minced garlic

¼ teaspoon chili powder

¼ teaspoon salt

½ teaspoon ground turmeric

1 tablespoon lemon juice

2 x 175 g (6 oz) plaice or sole fillets

vegetable oil, for shallow frying

1 tablespoon rice flour

1 tablespoon semolina

I first had this dish, kurmuri tali macchi, at my aunt's weekend resort in Goa and have never forgotten it. It makes a great snack or starter served with some fresh raita (see page 14).

Mix the ginger, garlic, chili powder, salt and ground turmeric with the lemon juice. Rub the mixture all over the fish fillets and leave for 5 minutes.

Heat the oil in a frying pan. Mix together the rice flour and semolina then dust or pat the fish with this mixture, pressing it onto the fish so that it sticks well. Shallow fry the fish for 2–3 minutes, then serve.

CHICKEN
WITH GREEN PEPPERS

serves four

3 teaspoons minced garlic

2 teaspoons garam masala

3 tablespoons vegetable oil

salt

4 skinless chicken breast fillets, each cut
   into 3 strips

2 cloves

2 green cardamom pods

2 bay leaves

1 teaspoon cumin seeds

2 small onions, sliced

1 teaspoon minced ginger

1 teaspoon ground turmeric

1 teaspoon chili powder

3 teaspoons ground coriander

200 g (7 oz) tomatoes, chopped

100 g (4 oz) green bell pepper strips

100 ml (3½ fl oz) light cream, plus extra
   to garnish

1 teaspoon sugar

1 tablespoon chopped fresh cilantro, plus
   extra to garnish

When I was growing up in India, green bell peppers were available only during the months of November, December and January. During that time we certainly had our fill of this dish, known as murgh simla mirch – now I can prepare it all year round.

Place the minced garlic, half of the garam masala, 1 tablespoon of the oil and 1 teaspoon of salt in a bowl and mix well. Add the chicken pieces and leave to marinate for about 2 hours.

Heat the remaining oil in a pan and add the cloves, cardamom pods, bay leaves and cumin seeds. When they begin to crackle add the sliced onions and fry for 10–15 minutes.

Add the minced ginger and the ground spices (except the remaining garam masala). Fry over a medium heat for 1 minute. Add the chopped tomatoes and continue to cook over a medium heat for 10 minutes. Add the green bell peppers and the cream. Add salt to taste then add the sugar and remaining garam masala. Cook for 2–3 minutes then add the chopped cilantro.

Cook the marinated chicken in a hot frying pan or under a preheated broiler for about 5–8 minutes each side. Arrange in a serving dish and pour the tomato and green pepper sauce over the top. Serve garnished with cream and plenty of chopped fresh cilantro.

OKRA WITH ONIONS

serves four

2 tablespoons vegetable oil, plus extra for
    deep-frying

350 g (12 oz) okra, diced

1 teaspoon cumin seeds

2.5 cm (1 in) piece of fresh ginger, chopped

4 cloves garlic, chopped

1 green chili, chopped

½ teaspoon ground turmeric

2 medium onions, sliced

1 tomato, diced

1 teaspoon ground cumin

juice of ½ lemon

salt

1 tablespoon chopped fresh cilantro

This very simple dish, known in India as bhendi do pyaaza, has become an all-time favourite in Indian restaurants.

Heat the oil for deep-frying in a large heavy-bottomed pan to 190°C (350°F). Add the okra and deep-fry for 5–8 minutes until it goes limp. Drain and set aside.

Heat the 2 tablespoons oil in another pan and add the cumin seeds. When they begin to crackle add the chopped ginger, chopped garlic, green chili and ground turmeric. After 1 minute add the sliced onions. Fry over a medium heat, stirring constantly, adding a little water to prevent sticking. Add the diced tomato.

When the onions have become soft but not coloured, add the deep-fried okra and stir well. Sprinkle with ground cumin, add the lemon juice and season with salt to taste. Finally, add the chopped cilantro and serve hot.

GINGERY TURNIPS

serves four

1 tablespoon vegetable oil

1 teaspoon cumin seeds

pinch of asafetida (optional)

1 teaspoon sesame seeds

2 green chilies, seeded and sliced

5 cm (2 in) piece of fresh ginger,
    peeled and cut into juliennes

450 g (1 lb) turnips, peeled and cut into
    wedges

1 teaspoon salt

½ teaspoon sugar

1 tablespoon lemon juice

pinch of ground nutmeg

Eaten very often in the northern state of Kashmir, this recipe can also be made with Savoy cabbage, raw beets, radish or zucchini instead of turnips. It can be eaten on its own, hot or cold, but it also works well as an accompaniment. It goes well with Smoked Lamb with Saffron (see page 112).

Heat the oil in a wok, karhai or large pan, then add the cumin seeds and asafetida, if using. When the cumin seeds start to crackle, add the sesame seeds. When they begin to brown add the green chilies, ginger and turnips. Cover and cook over a low heat for 15 minutes, stirring occasionally.

Add the salt, sugar and lemon juice. Cook for a further 2–3 minutes. Turn off the heat and sprinkle with nutmeg. Serve the turnips hot or cold.

Opposite: **Okra with onions**

SPICY SPINACH WITH EGGS

serves four

2 tablespoons vegetable oil

1 teaspoon black mustard seeds

1 onion, diced

2 cloves garlic, crushed

600 g (1 lb 5 oz) baby leaf spinach

1 tomato, diced

¾ teaspoon salt

¼ teaspoon chili powder

4 eggs

1 teaspoon black peppercorns, coarsely
   crushed

1 tablespoon chopped fresh cilantro

buttered bread or hot naan bread, to serve

This east Indian recipe is traditionally eaten for breakfast, brunch or lunch with naan bread or "pao", a type of soft bread roll.

Heat the oil in a shallow frying pan and fry the mustard seeds until they begin to crackle. Add the onion and garlic and sauté until the onion is translucent. Add the spinach, tomato, salt and chili powder. Cook, covered, over a medium heat for 10 minutes or until the spinach has wilted. Stir well and make four hollows in the spinach. Break an egg into each hollow. Cover and cook for another 10 minutes or until the eggs are set.

Sprinkle with black pepper and fresh cilantro. Lift the eggs and spinach out of the pan with a flat wooden spoon and slide onto a plate. Serve with buttered bread or hot naan bread.

TANGY FRUIT SALAD

serves two

1 tablespoon sherry

50 ml (2 fl oz) orange juice

1 teaspoon vegetable oil

½ teaspoon cumin seeds

1 cm (½ in) piece of cinnamon stick

4 cloves

4 green cardamom pods

½ pineapple, diced

1 red or green apple, chopped

handful red or green grapes, halved and
    seeded

1 tangerine or orange, segmented

1 green chili, seeded and chopped
    (optional)

pinch of ground nutmeg

This is a good snack if you are bored of eating just plain fruit and is a good example of how I like to add spice to just about everything! Surprisingly, a seeded green chili mixed in with the fruit gives this salad a pleasant "kick".

Mix the sherry and orange juice together in a large bowl.

Heat the oil in a small frying pan and then add the cumin seeds. When they begin to crackle add the cinnamon stick, cloves and cardamom pods. Turn off the heat and add this mixture to the sherry and orange juice. Toss in the fruit and the chili, if using, and sprinkle with nutmeg.

Dinner with the family at the end of the day is a key time for all of us to catch up on everyone's news. Although I am a busy working wife and mother, I strongly believe in the importance of cooking and eating a proper meal with my family. Many people still believe Indian food is time-consuming to prepare as well as being high in fat but this chapter is full of everyday dishes that are not only quick to prepare, but will provide a balanced diet. Choose from simple fish curries and meat dishes to crunchy vegetables and fresh salads.

everyday
family
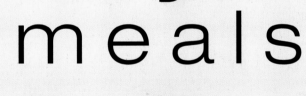

meals

FLAKY FLAT BREAD
WITH A SPICED EGG COATING

serves four

200 g (7 oz) all-purpose flour

200 g (7 oz) wholewheat flour

1 teaspoon ajowan (see page 122) or
   cumin seeds

1 tablespoon vegetable oil

150 ml (¾ cup) warm water

4 eggs, beaten

1 onion, finely chopped

1 tomato, finely chopped

1–2 green chilies, finely chopped

1 tablespoon chopped fresh cilantro

¾ teaspoon salt

3 tablespoons melted butter

lime pickle or tomato ketchup, to serve

This is commonly eaten by Indians for breakfast. Indian breads are made fresh every day and we were privileged as children to have a cook who spoilt us and served us the bread as it came hot off the griddle.

Combine the flours in a large bowl. Add the ajowan or cumin seeds. Rub the oil into the flour, then gradually add the water to make a pliable dough. Cover the bowl and let the dough rest for 20 minutes.

In a separate bowl, combine the eggs, onion, tomato, chilies, fresh cilantro and salt.

Using your hands, shape the rested dough into 8 balls of equal size. Roll out each ball on a floured board into a flat round of 12 cm (5 in) diameter.

Place each paratha on a preheated medium hot griddle or in a large frying pan and cook for 1–2 minutes on one side, spooning over a little melted butter at the edges. Turn over and cook for 1 minute on the other side, again spooning over a little melted butter at the edges. Flip over once again and spoon 2 tablespoons of the egg mixture on top, followed by ¹/₂ teaspoon of melted butter round the edges. Cook for 1 minute then flip over and again spoon 2 tablespoons of the egg mixture on top, followed by more melted butter round the edges. Cook until the egg is lightly set.

Serve the parathas hot with lime pickle or tomato ketchup.

Tip Shape the dough into 12 rather than 8 balls, if you require smaller parathas. These traditional Indian rolling pins are longer and thinner than western ones, however, a conventional rolling pin will work just as well.

MUSTARD **FISH** CURRY

serves four

4–6 x 150 g (5 oz) monkfish steaks

4 tablespoons Dijon mustard

3 tablespoons desiccated coconut

2 cloves garlic, crushed

1 tablespoon poppy seeds

1 onion, chopped

1 tablespoon vegetable oil

1 teaspoon black mustard seeds

100 ml (3½ fl oz) canned coconut milk

1 tablespoon ground coriander

2 teaspoons minced ginger

½ teaspoon salt

½ teaspoon sugar

2 tomatoes, diced

coarsely crushed black mustard seeds
   and watercress leaves, to garnish

This curry, known in India as reshmi rai maach, is absolutely heavenly served with steamed basmati rice and pappadums. The mustard seeds and watercress give it a lovely hot, peppery flavour.

Rub the monkfish steaks all over with the Dijon mustard.

Place the desiccated coconut, garlic, poppy seeds and onion in a food processor or blender and work until smooth, adding a little water if necessary to ease the blending.

Heat the oil in a pan. Add the mustard seeds and stir until they "pop" then add the blended mixture and fry gently for 2–3 minutes. Add the coconut milk, ground coriander, ginger, salt and sugar and cook for a further 10 minutes. Add the fish to the pan and cook for 5–8 minutes. Stir in the tomatoes and turn off the heat.

Sprinkle with coarsely crushed mustard seeds and watercress and serve hot.

AMRITSAR FISH CURRY

serves four

FOR THE BATTER

100 g (4 oz) chickpea flour (besan)

1 teaspoon minced garlic

1 teaspoon ground cumin

¼ teaspoon ground black pepper

½ teaspoon ground turmeric

½ teaspoon chili powder

75–100 ml (3–4 fl oz) water

FOR THE SAUCE

2 tablespoons vegetable oil

3 black peppercorns

½ teaspoon cumin seeds

2 bay leaves

1 onion, chopped

1 teaspoon minced garlic

1 teaspoon ground turmeric

1 teaspoon chili powder

1 teaspoon garam masala

3 teaspoons ground coriander

200 g (7 oz) tomatoes, chopped

2 green chilies, halved lengthways

1 tablespoon tamarind pulp

½ teaspoon sugar

salt

1 tablespoon chopped fresh cilantro

oil, for deep-frying

**300 g (11 oz) cod or haddock, cut into 4 cm
(1½ in) cubes**

Amritsar is a north Indian city in Punjab where fish is very seldom eaten – this recipe is a rare exception.

Mix together all the ingredients for the batter until you have a thick batter. Set aside.

To make the sauce, heat the oil in a pan and add the black peppercorns, cumin seeds and bay leaves. When they begin to crackle add the chopped onions and fry for 5–10 minutes.

Add the minced garlic, ground turmeric, chili powder, garam masala and ground coriander and fry for 1 minute. Add the chopped tomatoes and green chilies and continue to cook for 5–10 minutes. Add the tamarind pulp and cook for another 5 minutes. Lastly, add salt to taste, the sugar and half the fresh cilantro.

Heat the oil for deep-frying in a large heavy-based pan to 190°C (350°F).

Dip each cube of fish into the prepared thick batter, coating it evenly, then drop into the hot oil and deep-fry for about 5 minutes until golden brown.

Arrange the pieces of deep-fried battered fish on a serving dish and pour the sauce over the top. Serve hot, garnished with the remaining fresh cilantro.

FISH IN A **TANGY MINTY** SAUCE

serves four

4 large cod steaks, about 675 g (1½ lb)
   total weight
½ teaspoon garam masala
1 teaspoon salt
500 g (1¼ lb) chopped fresh cilantro
8–10 small radishes
2 large cloves garlic
2 green chilies, seeded
1 tomato, chopped
12–14 mint leaves
½ teaspoon minced ginger
1 tablespoon lemon juice
½ teaspoon sugar
1 tablespoon vegetable oil

This is an exceptional dish which is suitable not only as a quick tasty meal on a weekday but also for entertaining. If you are serving this for a dinner party, you can make the paste for the sauce in advance.

Smear the cod steaks with a mixture of garam masala, salt and fresh cilantro. Set aside for 12–15 minutes.

Put the remaining ingredients, except the oil, in a food processor or blender and blend to form a smooth paste.

Heat the oil in a deep frying pan. Cook the fish on each side for 3–4 minutes, then pour the puréed sauce mixture over the top. Cover and cook for 10 minutes over a medium heat. Serve while still hot.

CRISPY COCONUT PRAWNS
WITH TANGY MANGO SAUCE

serves four

2 tablespoons cornstarch
¾ teaspoon salt
½ teaspoon ground black pepper
750 g (1 lb 11 oz) raw king prawns (thawed
   weight if frozen), peeled and deveined
2 egg whites, lightly beaten
100 g (4 oz) desiccated coconut
vegetable oil, for deep-frying
FOR THE MANGO SAUCE
I ripe mango, peeled and chopped
3 tablespoons mayonnaise
3 tablespoons sweet mango chutney

Opposite: **Fish in a tangy minty sauce**

I am always tempted to make this recipe whenever I see king prawns at my local fishmonger's. It is great as a starter and absolutely delicious as a snack.

Season the cornstarch with the salt and pepper. Dust or toss the peeled king prawns in the cornstarch. Dip each prawn in the egg white and then roll in the desiccated coconut.

Heat the oil for deep-frying in a large heavy-bottomed pan to 190°C (350°F). While the oil is heating combine the ingredients for the mango sauce in a blender and work to a purée. Place in a serving dish.

When the oil is hot deep-fry a few prawns at a time for 2–3 minutes until golden or light brown. Keep warm while you cook the remaining prawns. Serve hot with the mango sauce.

DRY **SPICED** CHICKEN

serves four

2 tablespoons vegetable oil

1 teaspoon cumin seeds

½ teaspoon fennel seeds

1 bay leaf

2 medium onions, sliced

3 teaspoons ground coriander

1 teaspoon chili powder

1 teaspoon garam masala

1 teaspoon ground turmeric

350 g (12 oz) chicken, cut into 4 cm
    (1½ in) pieces

2 green chilies, halved lengthways

½ teaspoon black peppercorns, crushed

salt

1 tablespoon chopped fresh cilantro,
    to garnish

This is a great chicken dish for picnics as there is no sauce and therefore no fear of spillages. It has become a family favourite.

Heat the oil in a pan. Add the cumin seeds, fennel seeds and bay leaf. When they begin to crackle add the sliced onions and fry for 10–15 minutes over a low heat.

Add the ground coriander, chili powder, garam masala and ground turmeric. Sprinkle with a little water and continue to fry over a low heat.

Add the diced chicken and green chilies and fry, stirring continuously. Sprinkle with more water if required. Reduce the heat and cook, covered, for 10–15 minutes.

Add the crushed black peppercorns and salt to taste. Remove the lid and reduce any excess moisture by increasing the heat, stirring all the time. Serve garnished with fresh cilantro.

CHICKEN WITH **PEANUTS**

serves four

½ teaspoon whole fenugreek seeds

2 tablespoons vegetable or sunflower oil

900 g (2 lb) chicken thighs or drumsticks, skinned

1 large onion, chopped

1 tablespoon sesame seeds

1 teaspoon freshly cracked black pepper

1 teaspoon minced ginger

2 large tomatoes, chopped

1 tablespoon ground coriander

½ tablespoon ground cumin

¾ teaspoon ground turmeric

¾ teaspoon chili powder or paprika

200 g (7 oz) unsalted peanuts, shelled and skinned

1 teaspoon salt

½ teaspoon sugar

2 tablespoons green onions, chopped, to garnish (optional)

Although the Indian state of Gujarat is primarily vegetarian and has a large non-meat-eating community, there still remain some Muslims who eat meat in certain parts of this state. Groundnuts, or peanuts, grow plentifully and are eaten in a variety of dishes. Groundnut oil was traditionally used in this recipe but I use vegetable or sunflower oil instead.

Soak the fenugreek seeds in warm water for 15 minutes.

Heat the oil in a pan then sear the chicken until browned all over. Remove the chicken and drain on absorbent paper towels.

In the same oil, fry the onion and cook until translucent. Add the sesame seeds and cook until brown. Add the cracked black pepper, ginger, tomatoes, ground coriander, ground cumin, ground turmeric, chili powder and peanuts.

Return the chicken to the pan. Cover and cook for 20 minutes. You may need to add a little water if the chicken begins to stick to the pan.

Stir in the salt, sugar and soaked fenugreek seeds. Serve garnished with chopped green onions, if desired.

SPICED GROUND MEAT
WITH **SPINACH**

serves four

- 1 teaspoon vegetable oil
- 2–4 bay leaves
- 2–3 black cardamom pods, slightly opened
- 1 onion, sliced
- 450 g (1 lb) ground lamb or beef
- ½ teaspoon ground turmeric
- 1 teaspoon ground coriander
- 1 teaspoon minced ginger
- 1 tomato, chopped
- 1 teaspoon mint sauce, or 4–5 mint leaves
- ½ teaspoon ground cardamom
- 1 teaspoon garam masala
- 1 teaspoon salt
- ½ teaspoon sugar
- 300 g (11 oz) baby leaf spinach
- sliced fried onions, to garnish

Traditionally made with ground lamb or mutton, ground beef is now often substituted in this dish. It is commonly eaten throughout northern India. Serve the dish hot with pilau rice or naan bread.

Heat the oil in a pan. Add the bay leaves and black cardamom pods. After 2–3 seconds, add the sliced onion and cook until translucent. Add the ground lamb or beef, reduce the heat and cook for 10 minutes, stirring to brown the meat evenly. Add the ground turmeric, ground coriander, ginger and tomato.

Continue cooking, covered, for another 10 minutes. Add the mint sauce or mint leaves, ground cardamom, garam masala, salt and sugar. Stir well then fold the whole baby spinach leaves into the mince. Cover and cook for a further 3–4 minutes before serving, garnished with sliced fried onions.

GINGERED POTATOES
AND ONIONS

serves four

1 tablespoon vegetable oil

1 teaspoon black mustard seeds

1 teaspoon cumin seeds

450 g (1 lb) potatoes, peeled and diced

1 onion, cut into large dice

½ teaspoon ground turmeric

1 tablespoon ground coriander

1 teaspoon ground cumin

½ teaspoon chili powder

2.5 cm (1 in) piece of fresh ginger,
   peeled and cut into juliennes

1½ teaspoons salt

1 teaspoon sugar

1 tablespoon lemon juice

1 tomato, chopped, to garnish

chopped fresh cilantro, to garnish

This dish is a favourite throughout India, known as garam pyaz aloo. It is served with hot naan bread or chapattis. The heat levels can be reduced by using less chili and mustard seeds. Use any leftovers as a sandwich filling the next day – it is wonderful in toasted sandwiches.

Heat the oil in a wok or deep frying pan. Add the mustard seeds and stir until they "pop", then add the cumin seeds. When they begin to crackle add the diced potatoes, onion and all the ground spices. Cover, reduce the heat and allow to cook for 12–15 minutes. Add a little water if the vegetables start sticking to the pan.

Add the ginger, salt and sugar to the pan. Stir and cook for a further 3–4 minutes. Turn off the heat – the potatoes should be cooked by now. Stir in the lemon juice.

Garnish the dish with chopped tomato and cilantro leaves and serve.

DEEP-FRIED SPICED
NEW POTATOES

serves four

400 g (14 oz) new potatoes

vegetable oil, for deep-frying

¼ teaspoon chili powder

1 teaspoon ground roasted cumin seeds
   (see page 22)

juice of ½ lemon

1 tablespoon chopped fresh cilantro

½ teaspoon paprika

½ teaspoon sugar

salt and pepper, to taste (optional)

TO SERVE (OPTIONAL)

plain yogurt

Cilantro and Mint Raita (see page 13)

I make this when I have leftover cooked new potatoes – it makes a very good starter or accompaniment.

If you are using uncooked potatoes, boil them in their skins until they are cooked. Drain and allow to cool. When cool, hold each potato in your hands and press to flatten slightly.

Heat the oil for deep-frying in a large heavy-bottomed pan to 180°C (350°F). Add the potatoes to the hot oil and deep-fry for 10–15 minutes until golden brown and crisp.

Remove from the oil and drain on absorbent paper towels. Place in a bowl, add the remaining ingredients to the potatoes and mix well. Serve hot, drizzled with a little plain yogurt, if desired, and accompanied by Cilantro and Mint Raita.

SPICY SCRAMBLED EGGS

serves four

6 large eggs

50 ml (2 fl oz) milk

¼ teaspoon salt

1 tablespoon melted butter

1 tablespoon vegetable oil

1 teaspoon cumin seeds

1 green chili, diced

1 onion, finely diced

½ teaspoon minced ginger

¼ teaspoon ground turmeric

1 tomato, diced

2 tablespoons chopped fresh cilantro

1 tablespoon grated cheese

This is traditionally eaten for brunch. Originally a Persian dish, it is now served with an Indian "twist". The eggs can be served on top of toast or rolled into warm ready-to-eat chapattis, available from supermarkets.

Beat the eggs lightly in a bowl with the milk, salt and melted butter then set aside.

Heat the oil in a wok or deep frying pan. Sizzle the cumin seeds in the oil briefly then add the green chili, onion, ginger and ground turmeric and sauté lightly. Add the tomato and cook for a further 1–2 minutes. Add the egg mixture and cilantro and stir constantly for a few minutes until the eggs are cooked.

Serve the scrambled eggs hot, sprinkled with the grated cheese, on toast or in chapattis.

WHOLE OKRA
STUFFED WITH SPICES

serves four

300 g (11 oz) okra

1 teaspoon lemon juice

2 tablespoons vegetable oil

1 tablespoon chopped fresh cilantro, to
   garnish

FOR THE SPICE FILLING

25 g (1 oz) chickpea flour (besan)

1 teaspoon chili powder

1½ teaspoons salt

1 teaspoon sugar

1 teaspoon ground turmeric

3 teaspoons ground coriander

2 teaspoons ground cumin

50 g (2 oz) crushed peanuts

½ teaspoon asafetida

This dish is a speciality from the state of Gujarat on the western coast of India. Stuffing okra sounds fiddly but it is really a very simple recipe – the okra are baked in the oven leaving you time to prepare the rest of your meal.

Preheat the oven to 180°C (350°F), Gas 4.

   Clean the okra and make a slit along the length of each.

   Mix together in a bowl all the ingredients for the spice filling.

   Stuff the slits in the okra with the spice filling, then arrange the stuffed okra on a greased baking tray. Sprinkle the okra with the leftover spices, the lemon juice and the oil and cook in the preheated oven for 20–25 minutes until the okra is cooked.

   Serve hot, sprinkled with chopped fresh cilantro.

GARLIC-FLAVOURED LENTILS

serves four

200 g (7 oz) yellow lentils

½ teaspoon ground turmeric

salt

juice of ½ lemon

1 tablespoon pure ghee

½ teaspoon cumin seeds

3 cloves garlic, chopped

½ teaspoon crushed black peppercorns

2 tablespoons chopped fresh cilantro,
   to garnish

This dal comes from the Parsi community, based around Mumbai and Gujarat. I often eat it with biryani or on its own as a soup.

Wash the lentils in several changes of water. Boil in enough water to cover with the ground turmeric for about 20–25 minutes until the lentils are soft. Drain and allow to cool.

   Place the cooked lentils in a food processor or blender and work to a fine purée. Ensure that the lentils are of pouring consistency, adding a little more water if required. Reheat the lentil purée and add salt to taste and the lemon juice.

   In another small pan heat the ghee and add the cumin seeds, garlic and crushed black peppercorns. When they begin to crackle tip the spices over the lentils and mix well.

   Serve the lentils garnished with chopped fresh cilantro.

BABY CORN AND CRUNCHY GREEN BEANS

serves four

225 g (8 oz) green beans

1 teaspoon vegetable oil

1 teaspoon cumin seeds

1 green chili, seeded and chopped

200 g (7 oz) baby corn

½ teaspoon minced ginger

½ teaspoon salt

2 tablespoons water

2 tablespoons desiccated coconut

½ teaspoon garam masala

1 tablespoon chopped fresh cilantro

lemon juice, to serve (optional)

Many people think that Indian vegetable dishes have no texture because of the way that vegetables are cooked in many Indian restaurants outside of India. This dish undoes all those preconceptions!

Blanch the beans in a saucepan of boiling water for 2 minutes then drain. Slit lengthways. Top and tail the beans and cut each bean in half.

Heat the oil in a pan then add the cumin seeds. When they start to crackle, add the green chili. After 30 seconds add the green beans, corn, ginger and salt. Sprinkle with water. Reduce the heat, cover and cook for 3–4 minutes.

Uncover and sprinkle with the coconut, garam masala and fresh cilantro. Serve hot while the beans are still crunchy, sprinkling a little lemon juice on top if desired.

SPINACH WITH CARAMELIZED ONIONS AND SULTANAS

serves four

1 tablespoon vegetable oil

4 cloves

1 teaspoon cumin seeds

¼ teaspoon fenugreek seeds

1 red onion, sliced

¾ teaspoon brown sugar

1 tablespoon sultanas or other raisins

225 g (8 oz) baby spinach

½ teaspoon garam masala

salt

The first time I had this dish was in Agra, home of the Taj Mahal. Both the recipe and one of the most famous wonders of architecture left a lasting memory. If you wish, you can add a dash of cream before sprinkling with garam masala.

Heat the oil in a pan. Add the cloves and when they begin to swell add the cumin seeds and fenugreek seeds. When they begin to crackle add the sliced onion and brown sugar. Reduce the heat and cook the onion until browned.

Meanwhile, soak the sultanas in hot water for 2 minutes. Drain and add to the caramelized onions. Fold in the baby spinach. Sprinkle with garam masala and season to taste.

STEAMED FENNEL AND GREEN BEAN VERMICELLI

225 g (8 oz) dried vermicelli, broken into
   5 cm (2 in) lengths

100 g (4 oz) thawed frozen green beans,
   sliced

¾ teaspoon minced garlic

½ teaspoon minced ginger

½ teaspoon ground turmeric

3 green cardamom pods, cracked open,
   outer pods retained

2 teaspoons fennel seeds

1 onion, sliced

1 green chili, chopped

½ teaspoon vegetable oil

¾ teaspoon sugar

1 teaspoon salt

3–4 cloves

2.5 cm (1 in) piece of cinnamon stick

2 bay leaves

250 ml (8 fl oz) water

1 tablespoon chopped fresh cilantro

This accompaniment, known as saunf aur sem ki seviyan, is quite an unusual dish, and one that is not normally seen in Indian restaurants outside of India. I first tasted it in Baroda, a city in the state of Gujarat. It is a healthy option for those who are watching their weight.

Combine all the ingredients together in a large bowl and then place in a steaming basket or colander, large enough to fit inside a pressure cooker. Steam for 20–25 minutes. The vermicelli should have absorbed all the water.

Alternatively, put all the ingredients in a large glass bowl, cover and cook in the microwave on high for 15 minutes, or until all the water has been absorbed and the vermicelli is cooked.

Serve while still hot.

SPICY COUSCOUS SALAD

serves four

150 g (5 oz) couscous

10–12 cherry tomatoes, halved

7.5 cm (3 in) piece of cucumber, sliced

1 red onion, sliced

1 green chili, seeded

¾ teaspoon toasted cumin seeds

1 tablespoon chopped fresh cilantro

2 tablespoons lemon juice

½ teaspoon sugar

1 teaspoon salt

½ teaspoon ground black pepper

1 teaspoon olive, vegetable or sesame oil

Couscous has been eaten for several years in India but never in a salad. I experimented with leftover couscous to make this salad and was delighted with the result.

For an alternative version to the one below, drizzle the whole cherry tomatoes and the red onion with the oil and a little salt and roast in a preheated oven, 220°C (450°F), Gas 7, for 8–10 minutes. Add to the couscous along with the juices from the roasting dish and the remaining ingredients.

Cook the couscous according to the package instructions. Transfer to a large bowl and add all the remaining ingredients. Stir well to combine and serve at room temperature.

SPICED RICE

serves four

250 g (9 oz) basmati rice

3 tablespoons oil

¼ teaspoon cumin seeds

3 cloves

2 bay leaves

3 green cardamom pods

2 onions, sliced

1 tablespoon minced garlic

½ teaspoon ground turmeric

½ teaspoon chili powder

3 teaspoons ground coriander

200 g (7 oz) tomatoes, chopped

1½ teaspoons garam masala

2 tablespoons chopped fresh cilantro

salt

This spiced fragrant rice is a lunchtime dish but it could also be eaten as an accompaniment. Serve with plain yogurt.

Wash the rice in several changes of water then leave to soak for 10 minutes before draining well.

Heat the oil in a pan and add the cumin seeds, cloves, bay leaves and cardamom pods. When they begin to crackle add the sliced onions and fry over a medium heat for 5 minutes.

Add the minced garlic, ground turmeric, chili powder and ground coriander. Sprinkle with a little water and continue to cook over a low heat, stirring frequently. Add the tomatoes and continue to cook for 4–5 minutes. When the oil separates from the other ingredients, add the drained soaked rice. Add the garam masala and fresh cilantro and pour enough hot water into the pan to a level 1 cm (½ in) above the layer of rice. Add salt to taste and allow to cook over a medium heat.

When the water begins to boil, cover the pan. Reduce the heat and simmer for 10–12 minutes until the rice is cooked.

Opposite: **Spicy couscous salad**

TANGY CIRCLES OF **EGGPLANT**

serves four

**2 large purple eggplants, sliced into 1 cm
  (½ in) thick rounds**

1 teaspoon salt

1 tablespoon ground coriander

1 tablespoon ground cumin

¼ teaspoon ground turmeric

1 teaspoon minced garlic

2 tablespoons vegetable oil

1 teaspoon black mustard seeds

TO GARNISH

**1 teaspoon roasted coriander seeds,
  ground**

2 teaspoons chopped fresh cilantro

1 teaspoon lemon juice

*As a child khat mith baingan pati was one of my favourite
dishes – we used to beg to have this throughout November
and December as this was the only time of year that eggplants
were available. Now I can cook it any time – I like to serve it
with parathas (see page 12) or plain yogurt.*

Sprinkle the eggplant slices with the salt and set aside for
10–15 minutes. Gently squeeze each eggplant slice between the
palms of your hands to remove all remaining moisture.

   Mix together the ground coriander, cumin, ground turmeric
and minced garlic then sprinkle on both sides of the eggplants.

   Heat the oil in a wok. Add the mustard seeds and stir until
they "pop" then layer the eggplant in the pan, making sure that
each slice is slightly covered with the mustard oil.

   Cook for 3–4 minutes on one side then gently turn over with
a spatula to cook the other side. Do not cover the pan. Reduce
the heat and cook for 5 minutes. Turn off the heat.

   Serve, sprinkled with ground roasted coriander, fresh
cilantro and lemon juice.

BEANSPROUT AND PEANUT SALAD

serves four

1 teaspoon salt

800 g (1 lb 12 oz) beansprouts

100 g (4 oz) shelled peanuts or 200g (7 oz)
   snow peas or green beans

1 teaspoon tamarind pulp

2 tablespoons hot water

1 teaspoon vegetable oil

2 tablespoons sesame seeds

1 green chili, seeded and chopped

1 tablespoon pepper, coarsely ground

1 teaspoon minced ginger

2 tablespoons chopped fresh cilantro

salt and pepper, to taste

½ red onion, finely sliced, to garnish

This healthy salad is delicious eaten hot or cold. If you are allergic to nuts or on a diet, you can replace the peanuts with snow peas or whole green beans. Although beansprouts are most often used in Chinese cooking they are also used in northern parts of India.

Bring a large saucepan of salted water to the boil. Add the beansprouts and blanch for 2–3 minutes. Remove from the water using a slotted spoon and place in a large bowl.

Blanch the peanuts or green vegetables in the same water for 5 minutes. Drain then add to the bowl of beansprouts.

Stir the tamarind pulp and 2 tablespoons of hot water together to form a smooth paste. Set aside for 2–3 minutes.

Meanwhile, heat the oil in a pan then add the sesame seeds. When they start to crackle add the green chili and stir briefly. Add these spices to the beansprouts, then stir in the pepper, ginger, tamarind and fresh cilantro. Toss the salad and season to taste. Eat hot or cold, garnished with slices of red onion.

INDIAN CARROT PUDDING

serves four

2 tablespoons ghee

6–8 broken unsalted cashew nuts

10–12 raisins

1 kg (2¼ lb) carrots, peeled and grated

1 litre (1¾ pints) milk

75 g (3 oz) sugar

few drops of vanilla extract

pistachio slivers, to decorate

Known as gajjar halwa, this is India's favourite halwa. It can also be made with doodhi, a large Indian zucchini.

Heat the ghee in a pan and fry the cashew nuts and raisins over a low to medium heat. When they begin to colour add the grated carrots and sauté for about 5 minutes until the carrots are soft. Add the milk and bring to the boil, stirring well.

When the milk begins to boil, add the sugar. Reduce the heat to a simmer and cook for 15–20 minutes, by which time the milk will have reduced and the carrots turned mushy. Add the vanilla extract, turn off the heat and mix well. Serve either hot or cold, decorated with pistachio slivers.

easy entertaining

For me sitting down to enjoy some good food in the company of friends is one of life's greatest pleasures. This chapter is about simple entertaining and includes some of my favourite recipes. Some of the ingredients are a little more special while others, such as the spiced puffed bread, look fantastically impressive but these are all delicious recipes which can be prepared with the minimum of fuss.

MONKFISH WITH MUSHROOMS

serves four (as a starter)

1 tablespoon butter

4 cloves garlic, sliced

1 teaspoon minced ginger

8–10 green onions, chopped

1 green bell pepper, seeded and sliced

1 teaspoon chili powder

1 teaspoon salt

300 g (11 oz) monkfish, cut into 4 cm
(1½ in) cubes

12 raw king prawns, thawed if frozen,
peeled and deveined

50 g (2 oz) mushrooms, thickly sliced

2 tablespoons light cream

pinch of sugar

crushed black peppercorns, to garnish

I absolutely adore this starter. Monkfish and mushrooms both have a "meaty" texture and they complement each other well. Serve with a salad and some warm bread.

Heat the butter in a frying pan. Add the garlic, ginger, green onions, green bell pepper, chili powder and salt. Stir fry for 3–4 minutes then add the monkfish and prawns. Reduce the heat and continue frying for 5–7 minutes.

Add the mushrooms, cream and sugar. Cover the pan and simmer for 3–4 minutes. Sprinkle with crushed black pepper and serve hot.

FISH IN **FENNEL** AND CREAM

serves four

1½ tablespoons vegetable oil

75 ml (3 fl oz) whipping cream

¾ teaspoon salt

4 cloves garlic, finely crushed

1 tablespoon finely chopped fresh
cilantro

pinch of ground nutmeg

¼ teaspoon ground turmeric

4 x 150–175 g (5–6 oz) cod steaks

FOR THE PANCH POORAN SPICES

5 dried red chilies

1 teaspoon black mustard seeds

½ teaspoon fenugreek seeds

1½ tablespoons fennel seeds

1½ teaspoons cumin seeds

Panch pooran is a spice blend from Bengal with a powerful aroma. This east Indian delicacy will leave your taste buds tingling. The leftover panch pooran spices can be stored in an airtight container for up to six months. Serve the fish with rice and Mixed Vegetable Raita (see page 14).

Begin by mixing together all the panch pooran spices.

Place 1¹/₂ tablespoons of the prepared panch pooran spices in a bowl. Add the vegetable oil, double cream, salt, garlic, fresh cilantro, nutmeg and ground turmeric and mix well to form a paste. Rub this paste on both sides of the fish steaks and arrange the fish on a greased baking tray.

Place the fish under a preheated broiler and cook on one side for 5 minutes. Turn the fish over using a spatula and cook the other side for 3–4 minutes. Serve at once.

PRAWNS WITH SPINACH

serves four

2 tablespoons vegetable oil

½ teaspoon cumin seeds

2 bay leaves

1 large onion, chopped

1½ teaspoons minced ginger

4 cloves garlic, chopped

1 teaspoon ground turmeric

2 green chilies, chopped

½ teaspoon chili powder

2 tomatoes, diced

350 g (12 oz) raw prawns, peeled and
   deveined

150 g (5 oz) spinach, shredded

1½ teaspoons garam masala

2 tablespoons light cream

salt

2 tablespoons chopped fresh cilantro

Leafy vegetables, like the spinach in this recipe, are often combined with fish and meat in both the north and south of India. This is a great dish for entertaining – especially if you have guests who don't eat meat.

Heat the oil in a pan, add the cumin seeds and bay leaves. When they begin to crackle, add the chopped onion and fry for 5–8 minutes.

Add the minced ginger, garlic, ground turmeric and green chilies and continue to fry. Add the chili powder and diced tomatoes. After 2 minutes add the peeled prawns and cook for 5 minutes.

Add the shredded spinach, cover and allow to steam for 5 minutes to soften the spinach. Stir well. Add the garam masala and light cream and season to taste.

Stir in the chopped fresh cilantro and serve.

PRAWNS IN SWEET LIME CURRY WITH MANDARIN ORANGES

serves four

25 g (1 oz) butter

3 tablespoons vegetable oil

1 onion, very finely chopped

3 cloves garlic, chopped

1 teaspoon minced ginger

1 tablespoon ground coriander

1 teaspoon garam masala

6–8 curry leaves (optional)

2 chilies, finely chopped

1 kg (2¼ lb) large raw king prawns with
   tails on, peeled and deveined

2 tablespoons sweet lime pickle

100 ml (3½ fl oz) dry white wine

300 g (11 oz) can mandarin orange
   segments in juice, drained

salt

roughly chopped dill, to garnish

This is another great dish for a dinner party as the sauce can be made a day ahead. Simply add cooked prawns and heat through.

Heat the butter with the oil in a pan and fry the onion, garlic and ginger for 8–10 minutes until the onion is translucent.

Add the ground coriander, garam masala, curry leaves and green chilies. Continue cooking for 3–5 minutes. Add the prawns and cook, stirring gently, for 5 minutes. Stir in the lime pickle, dry white wine and drained mandarins. Adjust the seasoning to taste and cook for a further 3–5 minutes or until the sauce begins to thicken.

Serve the curry hot on a bed of plain steamed or boiled rice, garnished with dill.

Tip I find that a pinch of salt and sugar highlight the flavour.

BAKED GARLIC AND CHILI CHEESE OYSTERS

serves four (as a starter)

16 oysters, opened in their half shells

25 g (1 oz) butter

2 green onions (including green shoots),
   chopped

1 clove garlic, crushed

1 teaspoon very finely chopped fresh
   cilantro

2 teaspoons grated mild Cheddar or any
   blue-veined cheese if preferred

1½ teaspoon chili powder

The Indian name for this dish, samundar ka kamaal, always brings a smile to my face. Samundar means "sea" and kamaal means "fascination" or "wonder".

Preheat the oven to 150°C (300°F), Gas 2.

Rinse the oysters in cold water and place in a baking dish.

Heat the butter in a pan and add the green onions, garlic and cilantro. Mix well.

Spoon the green onion mixture over the oysters. Sprinkle with the cheese and chili powder and bake in the oven for 5–8 minutes or until the cheese starts to melt. Serve hot.

CHICKEN IN A STRONG
GARLIC SAUCE

serves four

3 tablespoons vegetable oil

2 cloves

2 green cardamom pods

2.5 cm (1 in) piece of cinnamon stick

½ teaspoon cumin seeds

1 large onion, sliced

2 teaspoons minced ginger

3 teaspoons minced garlic

½ teaspoon ground turmeric

½ teaspoon chili powder

1½ teaspoons ground coriander

200 g (7 oz) tomatoes, chopped

400 g (14 oz) chicken, cut into 2.5–4 cm
   (1–1½ in) cubes

2 tablespoons light cream

1 teaspoon garam masala

salt

5 cloves garlic, sliced

2 tablespoons chopped fresh cilantro, to
   garnish

*This chicken dish is a real must for garlic lovers! Garlic is
believed to have great curative powers, from aiding digestion
to guarding against infectious diseases.*

Heat 2 tablespoons oil in a pan and add the cloves, cardamom
pods, cinnamon and cumin seeds. When they begin to crackle,
add the sliced onions and fry for 5–10 minutes. Add the ginger,
garlic, ground turmeric, chili powder and ground coriander.
Reduce the heat and fry for 8–10 minutes.

Add the chopped tomatoes and continue to cook over a low
to moderate heat for 10–15 minutes.

Add the diced chicken and continue to cook for 10 minutes.
Sprinkle with a little water if the chicken is sticking to the pan.
Add the light cream and simmer for 5 minutes. Add salt to
taste and sprinkle with garam masala.

In another pan heat the remaining 1 tablespoon oil and fry
the sliced garlic over a moderate heat for 2–3 minutes until it
turns golden brown. Add to the chicken and serve the dish
garnished with fresh cilantro.

CHICKEN STUFFED WITH CASHEW NUTS, CHEESE AND PEAS

serves four

100 g (4 oz) cashew nuts, chopped or
    coarsely ground

200 g (7 oz) ricotta cheese

1 teaspoon cumin seeds

1 teaspoon garam masala

1 red onion, finely diced

100 g (4 oz) thawed frozen peas

½ teaspoon cracked black pepper

1 chili, seeded and finely chopped

½ teaspoon salt

4 skinned chicken breasts

FOR THE SAUCE

2 tablespoons butter

4 cloves

4 bay leaves

2.5 cm (1 in) piece of cinnamon stick

1 onion, chopped

1 teaspoon minced ginger

1 teaspoon finely chopped garlic

300 g (11 oz) canned chopped tomatoes

½ teaspoon ground turmeric

¼ teaspoon chili powder (optional)

½ teaspoon salt

1 teaspoon sugar

½ teaspoon garam masala

100 ml (3½ fl oz) light cream

The stuffing for this Indo-Persian dish can be made in advance and stored in the fridge until required.

Mix the cashew nuts, ricotta cheese, cumin seeds, garam masala, red onion, peas, black peppercorns, chili and salt together in a bowl.

Flatten the chicken breasts using a rolling pin or wooden mallet then spread a quarter of the nut mixture over each breast. Roll up each breast and secure with a toothpick or with meat string tied around each breast.

To make the sauce, heat the butter in a shallow pan. Add the cloves, bay leaves and cinnamon stick. When the cloves begin to "swell", add the onion, ginger and garlic and sauté for 5–7 minutes. Add the rolled stuffed chicken breasts to the pan and brown on all sides. Add a little water and cover the pan. Reduce the heat and cook for 15 minutes.

Add the tomatoes, ground turmeric, chili, salt, sugar and garam masala and let the chicken and tomato sauce simmer for 10–12 minutes, or until chicken is completely cooked.

Gently stir in the cream and serve the chicken hot with warm naan bread.

CHICKEN IN
ALMOND SAUCE

serves four

100 g (4 oz) flaked almonds, plus extra to
   garnish
2 tablespoons vegetable oil
1 teaspoon cumin seeds
3 cloves
3 green cardamom pods
1 teaspoon minced garlic
½ teaspoon ground turmeric
2 bay leaves
1 large onion, chopped
350 g (12 oz) chicken, cut into 2.5–4 cm
   (1–1½ in) cubes
50 ml (2 fl oz) light cream
1 teaspoon ground cardamom
1 teaspoon garam masala
1 teaspoon sugar
salt
1 tablespoon chopped fresh cilantro, to
   garnish

This is a great favourite with all my dinner guests, who often request this dish when they are invited – the fragrant creamy sauce is delicious. Serve with Spiced Kidney Beans with Ginger and Yogurt (see page 66).

Soak the flaked almonds in warm water for a couple of hours. Drain and then process in a food processor or blender to a fine purée. Set aside.

Heat the oil in a pan, add the cumin seeds, cloves, cardamom pods, minced garlic, ground turmeric and bay leaves. When the spices begin to crackle add the chopped onions and fry for 5–10 minutes.

Add the diced chicken and continue to fry, stirring continuously. Stir in the prepared almond purée. Cook over a low to medium heat for 15–20 minutes.

Stir in the light cream, ground cardamom and garam masala. Add the sugar and salt to taste. Cook for a further 3–5 minutes. Serve at once, garnished with a few almond flakes and chopped fresh cilantro.

Tip Why not try this recipe using other nuts? Pistachios, cashew nuts, pinenuts and chestnuts would all work well and give a completely different flavour.

PORK WITH
PICKLING SPICES

serves four

1 tablespoon vegetable oil

5 cm (2 in) piece fresh ginger, peeled
   and finely sliced

4 cloves garlic, finely chopped

450 g (1 lb) pork tenderloin, cut into 2.5 cm
   (1 in) strips

2 tablespoons sweet mango chutney

2 tablespoons hot lime pickle

2 tablespoons diagonally cut green shoots
   of green onion

1 teaspoon chopped fresh cilantro

This north Indian recipe lends itself to both special occasions and everyday cooking. It can be made with either pork or lamb. If using lamb, get the butcher to cut the meat from the leg into strips for you. Hot lime pickle is a popular condiment that can be found in Indian stores or supermarkets. Serve the meat with plain boiled basmati rice and lentils.

Heat the oil in a wok and gently fry the ginger and garlic for 1–2 minutes. Add the pork and stir-fry for 8–10 minutes. Add the mango chutney and hot lime pickle.

   Cover the pan, reduce the heat and cook for 5 minutes. Add a little water if the meat begins to stick. Turn off the heat, stir in the green onions and chopped fresh cilantro and serve.

LAMBS' LIVER
BAKED WITH **FENNEL**

serves four

2 tablespoons vegetable oil

500 g (1¼ lb) lambs' liver, cut into strips

2 tablespoons fennel seeds

20 g (¾ oz) creamed coconut

50 ml (2 fl oz) water

6 cloves garlic

1 small onion, finely chopped

1 teaspoon minced ginger

¼ teaspoon ground turmeric

¼ teaspoon black mustard seeds,
  coarsely crushed

¼ teaspoon asafetida (optional)

¾ teaspoon salt

Liver is not commonly eaten in India but this dish is a delicacy from the 1930s, which I was lucky enough to discover at a friend's house. Serve hot with green beans.

Preheat the oven to 180°C (350°F), Gas 4.

Heat the oil in a shallow frying pan. Sear the liver strips for 5–8 minutes and set aside.

Dry-fry the fennel seeds in a hot frying pan for 2–3 minutes, tossing them continuously. Coarsely crush with a rolling pin.

Combine the creamed coconut with the water and garlic. Boil in a pan for 5 minutes then put the mixture in a blender and work to a purée. Put the seared liver, the crushed fennel seeds, the coconut purée and all the remaining ingredients in an ovenproof dish. Cover with foil and bake in the oven for 25 minutes. Serve while still hot.

SPICED **KIDNEY BEANS**
WITH GINGER AND YOGURT

serves four

1 tablespoon vegetable oil or ghee

2.5 cm (1 in) piece of cinnamon stick

200 g (7 oz) plain yogurt

1 teaspoon minced ginger

8–10 green cardamom pods, crushed

¼ teaspoon ground turmeric

600 g (1 lb 5 oz) can kidney beans, drained

1½ teaspoons salt

¾ teaspoon chili powder

1 large tomato, chopped

TO GARNISH

1 tablespoon chopped fresh cilantro

1 tablespoon chopped onion

This rustic dish, known as rajma, is popular among all north Indian families, especially the farming community. It is a delicious accompaniment to Chicken in Almond Sauce (see page 62), or serve it simply with plain rice or naan bread and pappadums.

Heat the oil or ghee in a pan. Add the cinnamon stick and stir. After 2–3 seconds add the plain yogurt, ginger, crushed cardamom pods and ground turmeric. Cook over a medium heat, stirring constantly, for 10 minutes.

Add the remaining ingredients and cook for 15 minutes. Garnish with chopped cilantro and onion and serve.

LAMB AND POTATO CURRY

serves four

2 tablespoons vegetable oil

2 cloves

2 green cardamom pods

2 teaspoons ground black pepper

2 bay leaves

1 teaspoon cumin seeds

1 large onion, sliced

200 g (7 oz) tomatoes, chopped

1 teaspoon ground turmeric

1 teaspoon chili powder

1 teaspoon garam masala

3 teaspoons ground coriander

350 g (12 oz) lamb, cut into 4 cm (1½ in)
   cubes

150 g (5 oz) potato, cut into sticks

50 g (2 oz) plain yogurt

salt

chopped fresh cilantro, to garnish

Gosht aloo (lamb with potato) is an authentic recipe that is commonly eaten by non-vegetarian Indians. However, I have adapted it by adding a little yogurt to tone down the heat.

Heat the oil in a pan, add the cloves, cardamom pods, black pepper, bay leaves and cumin seeds. When they begin to crackle add the sliced onions and fry for 10–15 minutes over a medium heat until they turn translucent.

Add the chopped tomatoes, ground turmeric, chili powder, garam masala and ground coriander and continue to fry for a further 5 minutes.

Stir in the diced lamb, potato sticks and plain yogurt. Add salt to taste and cook, covered, over a low heat for about 20–25 minutes.

Serve hot, garnished with chopped fresh cilantro.

BABY CORN AND MUSHROOMS IN A SPICY TOMATO AND ONION SAUCE

serves four

2 tablespoons vegetable oil

½ teaspoon cumin seeds

2.5 cm (1 in) piece of fresh ginger, chopped

1 green chili, chopped

1 teaspoon ground turmeric

1 large onion, chopped

1 tablespoon minced garlic

½ teaspoon chili powder

2 teaspoons ground coriander

200 g (7 oz) tomatoes, chopped

1 teaspoon cumin seeds

1 teaspoon coriander seeds

1 teaspoon fennel seeds

½ teaspoon cracked black pepper

1 dried red chili, chopped

1 teaspoon sugar

salt

150 g (5 oz) baby corn, blanched for 2 minutes in boiling water and then cut lengthways

150 g (5 oz) mushrooms, blanched for 2 minutes in boiling water and then quartered

1 tablespoon light cream

1 tablespoon chopped fresh cilantro

This is known as tawa makai khumbh in India – a tawa is a heavy cast-iron griddle, traditionally used to make Indian breads like chapattis. This recipe has been adapted, however, so that it can be cooked in a wok or pan. This makes a good vegetarian main dish served with rice or bread, but I also like to eat it as an accompaniment to other dishes.

Heat the oil in a pan or wok and add the cumin seeds. When they begin to crackle add the chopped ginger, green chili, ground turmeric and onion in sequence and fry over a medium heat for 10 minutes.

Add the minced garlic, chili powder, ground coriander and chopped tomatoes and continue to cook for a further 5–10 minutes.

Meanwhile, in another pan dry-fry the cumin seeds, coriander seeds, fennel seeds, black pepper and chopped red chili over a low heat for 5 minutes. Transfer these spices to a mortar and crush to a coarse mix using the pestle. Sprinkle this mixture into the tomato sauce.

Add the sugar to the tomato sauce and salt to taste, then add the baby corn and mushrooms. Pour in the cream and cook for a further 2–3 minutes. Stir in the fresh cilantro and serve.

EGGPLANTS AND POTATOES

2 tablespoons vegetable oil

½ teaspoon cumin seeds

1 teaspoon minced ginger

1 green chili, chopped

4–5 curry leaves

½ teaspoon ground turmeric

½ teaspoon chili powder

¼ teaspoon asafetida

400 g (14 oz) tomatoes, chopped

150 g (5 oz) potatoes, diced

150 g (5 oz) eggplant, diced

salt

1 teaspoon sugar

1 tablespoon plain yogurt

chopped fresh cilantro, to garnish

I love eggplants and have a whole collection of recipes for this wonderful vegetable.

Heat the oil in a pan and add the cumin seeds. When they begin to crackle add the minced ginger, green chili and curry leaves. After 1 minute add the ground turmeric, chili powder and asafetida. Reduce the heat and sprinkle with a little water.

After about 2 minutes add the chopped tomatoes and bring to the boil. Add the potatoes and eggplant and cook, covered, at a simmer for 5–10 minutes. Check that the potatoes are cooked. Add salt to taste, stir in the sugar and yogurt.

Serve garnished with chopped fresh cilantro.

TAMARIND RICE

serves four

250 g (9 oz) basmati rice

3 tablespoons vegetable oil

2 tablespoons black mustard seeds

8–10 curry leaves

2 whole red chilies

1½ teaspoons asafetida (optional)

2 tablespoons sesame seeds

1½ teaspoons minced ginger

½ teaspoon ground turmeric

1 teaspoon salt

750 ml (1¼ pints) water

2 tablespoons tamarind pulp

200 g (7 oz) drained canned chickpeas,
   coarsely crushed

The combination of rice and tamarind pulp easily gives away that this is a dish from southern India. It is commonly served with fish dishes.

Wash the rice in several changes of water then leave to soak for 10 minutes before draining well.

Heat the oil in a large pan and fry the mustard seeds until they begin to crackle. Add the curry leaves, whole red chilies, asafetida and sesame seeds. As the sesame seeds begin to brown add the drained soaked rice, ginger and ground turmeric. Add the salt and water and bring to the boil.

Stir the tamarind pulp and crushed chickpeas into the rice mixture. Cover the pan and simmer for 15–20 minutes or until the rice is cooked. Serve at once.

Opposite: **Eggplants and potatoes**

SPICED DEEP-FRIED PURIS

serves four

400 g (14 oz) wholewheat flour

½ teaspoon salt

1 tablespoon vegetable oil

½ teaspoon ground turmeric

1 teaspoon ajowan seeds (see page 122)

½ teaspoon chili powder

150 ml (¼ pint) warm water

vegetable oil, for deep-frying

mango chutney, to serve

Puris are delicious rounds of dough that puff up when deep-fried. I often eat these as a snack with mango chutney but I also enjoy serving them to guests as they look very impressive.

Combine the flour and salt in a bowl and mix well. Rub the oil into the flour, then stir in the ground turmeric, ajowan seeds and chili powder. Slowly add the warm water into the spiced flour until it forms a pliable dough. Cover the bowl and set aside for 15–20 minutes.

Divide the rested dough mixture into 16 balls. Roll out each ball on a lightly floured surface into a 10 cm (4 in) round.

Heat the oil for deep-frying in a large heavy-bottomed pan until it is nearly smoking hot – 250°C (470°F). Once hot, reduce the heat to medium, about 180°C (350°F).

Immerse each puri one at a time in the hot oil. Gently push into the oil with a slotted spoon and allow to "puff up", which happens almost immediately. Turn once and cook the other side for 1–2 seconds. Remove from the pan using the slotted spoon and place on absorbent paper towels to drain while you cook the remaining puris.

Eat the puris while still puffed, with sweet mango chutney or any meat or vegetable dish.

SPINACH AND CHICKPEA FLOUR BREAD

serves four

250 g (9 oz) chickpea flour (besan)

50 g (2 oz) all-purpose flour

75 g (3 oz) spinach, shredded

½ teaspoon cumin seeds

1 cm (½ in) piece of fresh ginger, chopped

1 green chili, chopped

1 tablespoon chopped fresh cilantro

1 teaspoon ground turmeric

pinch of salt

4 tablespoons vegetable oil

This flat spiced bread with bright speckles of green spinach comes from the central states of India. Some people like to eat roti as soon as they are cooked, but I prefer them at room temperature.

Mix the chickpea flour in a bowl with the all-purpose flour and add all the other ingredients except the oil. Add enough water to make a thick dough. Use your hands to work the spinach well into the dough.

Divide the dough into 8 and roll out each piece on a floured board into a flat round of 12–15 cm (5–6 in) diameter.

Heat a pancake pan or griddle. Cook the flat breads one at a time for 2–3 minutes on each side then turn over and cook the other side. Drizzle with oil and continue to cook until the breads are well done, turning the bread over frequently during cooking.

BEET PUDDING

serves four

150 g (5 oz) boiled beets, diced

1 litre (1¾ pints) milk

100 g (4 oz) sugar

1 tablespoon rice flour

2 tablespoons ghee

10–12 raisins

10–15 unsalted cashew nuts, roughly chopped

few drops of rose essence

rose petals, to decorate

One would probably never imagine combining milk with beets, but it makes a vibrant dessert and looks lovely when decorated with rose petals.

Place the boiled beets in a food processor. Add a little water and blend to a fine purée.

Pour the milk into a saucepan and bring to the boil. Reduce the heat and simmer for 15–20 minutes. Add the sugar and stir well to dissolve.

Mix the rice flour in a cup with a little water to make a paste. Add this paste to the milk, stirring the mixture continuously as it starts to thicken.

In another pan heat the ghee and add the raisins and cashew nuts. Fry for 1–2 minutes. Add the beet purée and cook for 10–12 minutes over a low heat.

Pour the beet mixture into the thickened milk and mix well to obtain an even pink colour. Add the rose essence and pour into 4 individual dessert cups.

Serve chilled, decorated with a few rose petals.

COOL **MANGO** SOUP

makes 1.8 litres (3 pints)

4 large semi-ripe mangoes

1.5 litres (2½ pints) water

8–10 tablespoons brown sugar

1 tablespoon minced ginger

1 teaspoon ground black pepper

1 teaspoon chat masala (see page 122)

1 teaspoon coarsely crushed roasted cumin seeds (see page 22)

1 teaspoon salt, or to taste

Mangoes are Indians' favourite fruit and we try to make as many recipes with them as possible during the mango season, which in India runs from March until May. They are grown in abundance in Mumbai, where I grew up.

This recipe is a drink or soup, which is mainly prepared in Gujarat households and sipped throughout the sultry heat of the day to keep one cool. Once made, it keeps for up to 4 days in the fridge.

Peel the mangoes and cut them into big chunks. Do not discard the pits.

Boil the mango pieces and pits in the water for 15 minutes, or until the mango turns pulpy. Leave to cool.

Discard the mango pits. Put the mango flesh in a blender and work to a purée. Return to the saucepan and bring back to the boil. Add the remaining ingredients.

The "soup" is best served cold with ice or at room temperature.

Tip Add a little extra sugar if the raw mangoes are very tangy.

home
comforts

Some days I just want to curl up on the sofa and indulge in some comfort food. For me, this can be anything from a bowl of spicy pumpkin soup to a delicious, warming dal. In this chapter I have included some of my family's favourite dishes, from the dry spiced cabbage dish which my daughter loves to fried sweet potatoes with ice cream. Enjoy.

CHICKPEA FLOUR PANCAKES

serves four

250g (9 oz) chickpea flour (besan)

pinch of salt

½ teaspoon ground turmeric

¼ teaspoon baking soda

½ teaspoon ground cumin

1 tablespoon plain yogurt

1 onion, finely chopped

1 green chili, finely chopped

2 tomatoes, diced

1 tablespoon chopped fresh cilantro

4–5 tablespoons vegetable oil

Known as cheela, these thick pancakes are eaten throughout northern and central India, both as a breakfast dish and as a snack with pickles and mango chutney.

Put the flour in a bowl. Add the salt, ground turmeric, baking soda, ground cumin, yogurt and enough water to make a slightly thick flowing batter. Stir in the chopped onion, green chili, tomatoes and cilantro.

Heat a non-stick 12 cm (5 in) pancake pan. Pour in a little of the batter, spreading it to cover the base completely and make a thin pancake. Drizzle 1 teaspoon oil over the top.

Reduce the heat and continue to cook the pancake for about 2–3 minutes. Turn the pancake over and cook the other side for 2–3 minutes. Remove from the pan and keep warm while you make another 7 pancakes in the same way. Serve hot.

MEENA PATHAK'S
PUMPKIN SOUP

serves four

1 tablespoon butter

4 green onions, finely chopped

675 g (1½ lb) pumpkin, peeled and cut
  into 1.5-2 cm (¾ in) cubes

2 carrots, diced

1 teaspoon salt

¾ teaspoon ground black pepper

¼ teaspoon ground green cardamom

¼ teaspoon ground cinnamon

¼ teaspoon ground cloves

pinch of ground nutmeg

300 ml (½ pint) vegetable stock

100 ml (3½ fl oz) milk

50 ml (2 fl oz) light cream

2 tablespoons finely chopped dill leaves,
  to garnish

Often called MKP's pumpkin soup in my family, this came about when I was trying to use up some leftover vegetables in the fridge. It has become the family's favourite soup.

Heat the butter in a large saucepan. Add the green onions and sauté for 3–4 minutes.

Add the pumpkin, carrots, salt and all the ground spices and stock. Bring to the boil. Cook until the carrots and pumpkin are cooked – about 10–15 minutes.

Allow the mixture to cool slightly before putting it in a blender. Give it a couple of bursts of power, but do not purée it down completely.

Return the mixture to the pan. Add the milk and bring back to the boil. Stir in the cream, adjust the seasoning to taste, and serve hot, garnished with dill leaves.

EASY GRILLED CHICKEN BITES

serves four

1 tablespoon paprika

2 teaspoons garam masala

1½ teaspoons salt

1 teaspoon sugar

1 tablespoon vegetable oil, plus extra for
   drizzling

1 tablespoon minced garlic

1 tablespoon plain yogurt

250 g (9 oz) skinless chicken breast fillets,
   cut into bite-sized pieces

TO GARNISH

onion, cut into rings

1 tablespoon chopped fresh cilantro

few sprigs of mint

This is a classic starter that you would expect to find in a north Indian non-vegetarian household – however I often make these as a snack for my family.

Combine all the ingredients except the chicken together in a bowl and mix well. Add the chicken and mix well, ensuring that the marinade coats all the chicken pieces. Set aside to marinate for a few minutes.

Place the chicken pieces in a grill pan and drizzle with a little oil. Place under a preheated medium broiler and cook for 5–8 minutes until golden brown. Turn the pieces over and cook the other side for another 5 minutes.

When cooked, remove and arrange on a plate. Serve with onion rings, chopped cilantro and mint sprigs.

DEVILLED PRAWNS

serves four

1 tablespoon vegetable oil

1 onion, finely chopped

2 cloves garlic, finely chopped

¾ teaspoon chili powder

1 teaspoon paprika

¼ teaspoon ground black pepper

¼ teaspoon ground turmeric

½ teaspoon grated fresh ginger

1 teaspoon salt

750 g (1 lb 11 oz) peeled raw prawns
   (thawed weight if frozen)

150 ml (¼ pint) water

1 tablespoon tomato ketchup

These delicious spicy prawns are great for cold wintry nights. Serve the prawns hot with naan bread or on crackers with Cilantro and Mint Raita (see page 13).

Heat the oil in a wok or heavy-bottomed frying pan. Add the onion and cook until golden brown. Add the garlic, chili powder, paprika, black pepper, ground turmeric, ginger and salt. Cook, stirring, for 2–3 minutes.

Add the prawns and cook for 5 minutes. Then add the water, cover and bring to the boil. Stir in the tomato ketchup and cook, uncovered, for 2–3 minutes, before serving hot.

TANDOORI
GRILLED VEGETABLES

serves four

1 large green bell pepper, seeded and
   sliced

1 large red bell pepper, seeded and sliced

4 large tomatoes, sliced

1 large onion, sliced

2 zucchini, sliced

10–12 mushrooms

1–2 green chilies, seeded and sliced

½ teaspoon salt

½ teaspoon ground black pepper

2 tablespoons vegetable or olive oil

½ teaspoon ground turmeric

1 teaspoon ground cumin

1 teaspoon ground coriander

10–12 black olives, pitted

10–12 capers

8–10 fresh basil leaves

1–2 teaspoons chopped fresh cilantro

FOR THE DRESSING

100 g (4 oz) plain yogurt

2 tablespoons honey

2 tablespoons tomato paste

1 tablespoon vegetable oil

½ teaspoon minced garlic

½ teaspoon minced ginger

salt

*There are some days when I don't want to eat any meat or fish
and it is then that I find this dish satisfying and nutritionally
healthy. It is a versatile recipe to which one can add any
favourite vegetables or eliminate anything that is not liked.
This is my personal version. It makes a good accompaniment to
Blackened Spiced Cod (see page 83), or serve it simply with
naan bread and pappadums.*

Preheat the oven to 180–200°C (350–400°F), Gas 4–6.

Put all the ingredients for the dressing into a blender, add
salt to your taste and blend to a smooth paste. Set this aside
until the vegetables are ready.

Spread the vegetables evenly on a baking tray. Mix together
the salt, pepper, oil, ground turmeric, ground cumin and ground
cilantro and stir into the vegetables with a wooden spoon.
Sprinkle with the olives, capers, basil leaves and fresh cilantro.

Cook the vegetables under a preheated broiler for
10–12 minutes. Turn off the broiler and place the vegetables in
the oven for 5–7 minutes.

Serve hot drizzled with the prepared dressing.

BLACKENED SPICED COD

serves four

1 tablespoon fennel seeds

1 teaspoon mustard seeds

1 teaspoon cumin seeds

2.5 cm (1 in) piece of cinnamon stick

1 teaspoon ground turmeric

½ teaspoon ground black pepper

1 teaspoon minced ginger

1 teaspoon salt

4 x 150–175 g (5–6 oz) thick cod fillets,
    skin on

2 tablespoons vegetable oil

FOR THE SAUCE

1 teaspoon butter

40 ml (1½ fl oz) orange juice

1 tablespoon chopped fresh cilantro

1 green chili, finely chopped (optional)

This dish is a speciality from Mumbai (formerly Bombay), the city where I was born. Cod is my favourite fish for this recipe but you could also use sea bass, haddock or even skate. Serve it hot with a plain green salad or Tandoori Grilled Vegetables (see page 81) and pappadums.

Put the fennel seeds, mustard seeds, cumin seeds and cinnamon in a coffee grinder and blend to a fine powder. Mix the ground turmeric, black pepper, ginger and salt into this mixture.

Dust each fish fillet with this blend of spices. Heat the oil in a non-stick frying pan and sear the fish for 2-3 minutes on each side. Place in a serving dish and set aside.

Make the sauce by heating the butter in a pan with the remaining ingredients. Bring to the boil then pour over the fish and serve while still hot.

INDIAN FRIED FISH

serves four

1 teaspoon ground turmeric

¾ teaspoon chili powder

2 teaspoons minced ginger

1 teaspoon lemon juice

1 teaspoon ground coriander

1 teaspoon ground cumin

1 teaspoon salt

½ teaspoon asafetida (optional)

4 x 150–175 g (5–6 oz) cod or haddock fillets

FOR THE COATING

4 tablespoons chickpea flour (besan)

1 tablespoon rice flour

¾ teaspoon salt

½ teaspoon ground turmeric

1 teaspoon garam masala

vegetable oil, for frying

1 egg, beaten

In India something as simple as fried fish can be made exotic, as this recipe demonstrates. Serve it hot with plain rice, Gujarati Dal (see page 95) and lime pickle or have it as a snack that you can eat with your fingers.

Combine the ground turmeric, chili powder, ginger, lemon juice, ground coriander, ground cumin, salt and asafetida together in a small bowl.

Dry the fish on absorbent paper towels and smear both sides of each piece with the blended spice mixture. Set aside for 15 minutes to enable the flavours to penetrate.

Meanwhile combine all the dry ingredients for the coating, and pour the oil for frying into a shallow frying pan – enough to cover the base of the pan.

Heat the oil. Take each fish fillet, dip it into the beaten egg and then coat with the spiced flour. When the oil is hot shallow fry each piece of fish for 3 minutes on one side. Turn over and fry for another 2 minutes.

Drain on absorbent paper towels before serving hot.

SPICED CHICKEN IN A
TOMATO AND MINT SAUCE

serves four

4 skinned chicken breasts

150 g (5 oz) plain yogurt

1 tablespoon ground coriander

1 tablespoon ground cumin

½ teaspoon ground turmeric

½ teaspoon salt

1 teaspoon green chili, minced

6 tablespoons breadcrumbs

5 tablespoons vegetable oil or butter

FOR THE SAUCE

2 tablespoons vegetable oil

1 onion, finely chopped

3 cloves garlic, finely chopped

400 g (14 oz) canned chopped tomatoes

2 tablespoons finely chopped mint leaves

1 tablespoon garam masala

¾ teaspoon ground turmeric

1 teaspoon chili powder or dried chili
   flakes

1 teaspoon sugar

1 teaspoon salt

TO SERVE

Cilantro and Mint Raita (see page 13)

naan bread

When my children have friends over I sometimes make this chicken without the sauce and serve it as a spicy chicken burger, with a mango chutney and mayonnaise spread.

Preheat the oven to 180°C (350°F), Gas 4.

Flatten the chicken breasts with a mallet.

Mix together the yogurt, ground coriander, ground cumin, ground turmeric, salt and green chili. Marinate the chicken breasts in this mixture for 20–25 minutes at room temperature.

Tip the breadcrumbs onto a shallow plate. Lift each chicken breast out of the marinade and gently coat with the breadcrumbs. Heat the vegetable oil or butter in a pan and gently shallow-fry the coated chicken, two at a time, for 5–7 minutes on each side over a medium heat. Remove from the frying pan and place on a greased baking tray. Bake the chicken in the oven for 15 minutes or until completely cooked.

Meanwhile, in another shallow pan, heat the oil for the sauce. Sauté the onion and garlic until golden brown. Add the canned tomatoes, mint leaves, garam masala, ground turmeric, chili powder or dried chili flakes, sugar and salt. Cover and simmer for 10 minutes.

Transfer the cooked chicken into the sauce, cover and cook for a further 5 minutes. Drizzle with a little raita and serve hot with naan bread.

CHICKEN WITH GREEN ONIONS

2 tablespoons vegetable oil

1 teaspoon cumin seeds

1 onion, chopped

1 teaspoon minced garlic

½ teaspoon ground turmeric

2 teaspoons ground coriander

½ teaspoon chili powder

250 g (9 oz) tomatoes, chopped

50 g (2 oz) green onions, chopped

350 g (12 oz) chicken, cut into 2.5–4 cm
   (1–1½ in) cubes

1 teaspoon fennel seeds

1 teaspoon coriander seeds

½ teaspoon ground black pepper

½ teaspoon crushed red chilies

50 ml (2 fl oz) light cream

½ teaspoon dried fenugreek leaves

1 tablespoon chopped fresh cilantro

1 teaspoon sugar

salt

chopped green onions, to garnish

My family loves onions and this recipe reflects their passion for them. I like to cook this when we're all spending an evening at home together.

Heat the oil in a pan and add the cumin seeds. When they begin to crackle add the chopped onion and fry for 10–15 minutes over a medium heat.

Add the minced garlic, ground turmeric, ground coriander and chili powder. Fry for 1 minute then add the chopped tomatoes. Continue to cook for 5–10 minutes before adding the green onions and chicken pieces. Cook over a medium heat for 15 minutes, stirring occasionally.

In another pan dry-fry the fennel seeds, coriander seeds, black pepper and red chilies for 5–8 minutes then crush using a mortar and pestle.

Add the crushed spice mix to the sauce together with the cream, fenugreek leaves and chopped fresh cilantro. Add the sugar and salt to taste.

Serve hot, garnished with chopped green onions.

SLOW-COOKED CHICKEN
WITH BABY ONIONS

serves four

3 tablespoons vegetable oil

10–12 baby onions or shallots, peeled

2 green chilies, halved lengthways

8–10 curry leaves

2 onions, chopped

3 cloves garlic, crushed

1 teaspoon minced ginger

2 teaspoons ground coriander

1 teaspoon chili powder

½ teaspoon paprika

500 ml (17 fl oz) water or chicken stock

1 teaspoon salt

1 kg (2¼ lb) skinned chicken thighs or
    drumsticks

½ teaspoon sugar

TO GARNISH

1 teaspoon chopped fresh mint

1 tablespoon chopped fresh cilantro

1 tomato, chopped

The Indian name for this dish, pyaz aur murgh ki haandi, tells you that it was traditionally made in an earthenware pot (haandi). If you don't have one you can use a slow cooker, crockpot or casserole dish.

Heat the oil in a large, flame-proof casserole dish or in a saucepan. Sauté the baby onions or shallots gently for 2–3 minutes. Remove from the pan and place on absorbent paper towels.

Using the same oil fry the chilies, curry leaves and chopped onions for 5 minutes, or until the onions are light brown in colour and slightly translucent. Add the garlic, ginger, ground coriander, chili powder, paprika, water or chicken stock and salt. Bring to the boil and add the chicken. Reduce the heat and cook, uncovered, for about 20–30 minutes.

Return the sautéed baby onions to the pan, together with the sugar. Stir and cook for a further 3–4 minutes.

Garnish with the mint, fresh cilantro leaves and chopped tomato and serve hot with chapattis or naan bread.

RICE WITH GROUND LAMB

serves four

150 g (5 oz) basmati rice

50 ml (2 fl oz) vegetable oil

2 cloves

2 green cardamom pods

2 x 2.5 cm (1 in) pieces cinnamon stick

½ teaspoon cumin seeds

1 onion, chopped

1 tablespoon minced garlic

200 g (7 oz) tomatoes, chopped

1 teaspoon ground turmeric

½ teaspoon chili powder

4 teaspoons ground coriander

2 teaspoons garam masala

250 g (9 oz) ground lamb

2 green chilies, halved lengthways

100 g (4 oz) potatoes, peeled and diced

1 tablespoon fresh mint, chopped

1 tablespoon chopped fresh cilantro

salt

FOR THE DOUGH (TO SEAL THE VESSEL)

flour, as required

water, as required

The Indian name for this recipe is dum kheema pulav, which translates as "rice cooked with minced lamb in a sealed vessel". A traditional mince recipe from the north-west of India, it is not as difficult to make as it sounds. Serve it hot with a fresh yogurt raita. For me, this is comfort food at its best – a one-pot dish that is perfect for cold wintry nights.

Preheat the oven to 200°C (400°F), Gas 6.

Wash the rice in several changes of water then leave to soak for 10 minutes before draining well.

Heat the oil in an ovenproof pan that has a lid and add the cloves, cardamom pods, cinnamon and cumin seeds. When they begin to crackle add the chopped onions and fry over a medium heat for 5-10 minutes.

Add the minced garlic, chopped tomatoes and the ground spices and stir well. Stir in the ground lamb and green chilies and continue to cook. After about 5 minutes, add the drained soaked rice, potatoes and fresh herbs and mix well.

Add enough hot water to cover the rice plus a little extra – approximately 1 cm (½ in) over the level of rice. Add salt to taste. Bring to the boil then remove from the heat.

Make a thick dough using just flour and water. Roll out to a long sausage-shape strip and use it to seal the space between the pan and its lid to prevent any air getting into the pan.

Place the ovenproof pan in the oven and cook for about 30–45 minutes. Remove the dough and lid and serve the lamb hot.

LAMB IN A CASHEW NUT AND MINT SAUCE

serves four

100 g (4 oz) cashew nuts

2 tablespoons vegetable oil

2 cloves

2 green cardamom pods

2 bay leaves

½ teaspoon cumin seeds

1 large onion, chopped

1½ teaspoons minced garlic

1 teaspoon minced ginger

150 g (5 oz) tomatoes, chopped

2 teaspoons ground coriander

½ teaspoon ground turmeric

350 g (12 oz) lamb, cut into 2.5–4 cm
 (1–1½ in) cubes

100 ml (3½ fl oz) light cream

2 tablespoons chopped mint, plus a few
 extra leaves to garnish

1 tablespoon chopped fresh cilantro

1 teaspoon sugar

salt

This dish came about by accident when I was defrosting the fridge one day and had to use up the contents of the fridge for the evening meal. Now I make it by popular demand.

Soak the cashew nuts in hot water for 2–3 hours, drain and then work in a blender to a fine paste. Set aside.

Heat the oil in a pan and add the cloves, cardamom pods, bay leaves and cumin seeds. When they begin to crackle add the chopped onions and fry over a medium heat for 8–10 minutes.

Add the minced garlic, minced ginger, chopped tomatoes, ground coriander and ground turmeric. Cook for another 5 minutes, stirring constantly.

Stir the cashew nut paste into the mixture and continue to cook for another 5 minutes.

Add the diced lamb. Reduce the heat and leave to cook, covered, for 30 minutes.

Stir in the light cream, chopped mint, cilantro and sugar and adjust the seasoning to taste. Serve hot, garnished with a few mint leaves and accompanied by some plain basmati rice (see page 12).

DRY SPICED CABBAGE

serves four

1½ tablespoons vegetable oil

½ teaspoon mustard seeds

½ teaspoon cumin seeds

¼ teaspoon asafetida

½ teaspoon ground turmeric

5–6 curry leaves

1½ teaspoons minced ginger

1 green chili, chopped

1 dried red chili

350 g (12 oz) cabbage, shredded

75 g (3 oz) carrots, grated

1 teaspoon sugar

salt

juice of ½ lemon

1 tablespoon chopped fresh cilantro

My daughter adores this vegetable dish – she always requests it when she is feeling under the weather! The lemon juice and fresh cilantro give it a lovely fresh taste.

Heat the oil in a pan and add the mustard seeds and cumin seeds. When they begin to crackle add the asafetida, ground turmeric, curry leaves, ginger and chilies. Stir in the shredded cabbage and carrots.

Reduce the heat, cover the pan and allow to cook for about 15–20 minutes. Add the sugar and salt to taste. Sprinkle with lemon juice and chopped cilantro and serve hot or cold.

OKRA IN YOGURT

serves four

250 ml (8 fl oz) water

350 g (12 oz) thick plain yogurt

50 g (2 oz) sugar

1½ teaspoons minced ginger

1 green chili, chopped

1 tablespoon chickpea flour (besan)

pinch of salt

2 tablespoons vegetable oil, plus extra for
   deep-frying

15 okra, sliced into rounds

½ teaspoon cumin seeds

½ teaspoon mustard seeds

pinch of asafetida

6 curry leaves

chopped fresh cilantro, to garnish

This Gujarati okra dish is a great accompaniment to Kitcheri (see page 95).

Mix the water and yogurt together in a bowl. Stir in the sugar, ginger, green chili, chickpea flour and a pinch of salt and keep whisking until the chickpea flour blends into the yogurt.

Heat the oil for deep-frying in a large heavy-bottomed pan to 190°C (350°F). Add the okra and fry for 5–8 minutes.

In another pan heat the 2 tablespoons oil, add the cumin seeds, mustard seeds, asafetida and curry leaves. When the mustard seeds begin to crackle reduce the heat and pour the yogurt mixture into the pan. Cook for about 10–15 minutes until the yogurt begins to boil.

Add the deep-fried okra to the sauce, sprinkle with chopped fresh cilantro and serve.

Opposite: **Dry spiced cabbage**

KITCHERI

serves four

400 g (14 oz) basmati rice

300 g (11 oz) red lentils

300 g (11 oz) green split lentils

2 teaspoons vegetable oil

4 cloves

1 teaspoon cumin seeds

1–2 green chilies, chopped

4–5 bay leaves

2–3 garlic cloves, finely chopped

1 onion, sliced

1 large carrot, diced or sliced

100 g (4 oz) thawed frozen peas

1 litre (2 pints) hot water

2 teaspoons salt

1 teaspoon ground turmeric

1 tablespoon cracked black pepper

1 tablespoon butter

This is a great winter dish, especially when your spirits are low and you don't want to cook an elaborate meal. It is an all-time favourite with my family! The texture of kitcheri is very like stodgy porridge, and it is best served with a spicy salad, Okra in Yogurt (see page 92) or plain yogurt and pappadums.

Mix the rice and lentils together in a large pan or bowl and rinse in several changes of water. Drain well.

Heat the vegetable oil in a large pan and add the cloves and cumin seeds. When the cumin seeds begin to crackle and the cloves begin to swell add the green chilies and bay leaves, followed immediately by the garlic, onion, carrot and green peas, washed lentils and rice mixture, hot water, salt, ground turmeric, black pepper and butter.

Reduce the heat and cook until the rice and lentils are cooked – approximately 20–25 minutes.

GUJARATI DAL

serves four

250 g (9 oz) yellow lentils

1 teaspoon ground turmeric

1½ teaspoons jaggery or brown sugar

1 tablespoon vegetable oil

2 cloves

2 green cardamom pods

½ teaspoon cumin seeds

½ teaspoon mustard seeds

2 bay leaves

½ teaspoon asafetida

juice of ½ lemon

chopped fresh cilantro, to garnish

Opposite: **Gujarati dal**

This is one of my favourites – a good dal can really revive the spirits!

Wash the yellow lentils in several changes of water. Put in a pan with four times their quantity of water. Add the ground turmeric and boil for 30 minutes until the lentils are mushy.

Add the jaggery or brown sugar and a little salt to taste.

In another pan, heat the oil and add the cloves, cardamom pods, cumin seeds, mustard seeds, bay leaves and asafetida. Reduce the heat. When the seeds begin to crackle pour the mixture over the cooked lentils and stir well.

Stir in the lemon juice and sprinkle with chopped fresh cilantro to garnish.

GOAN RICE

500 g (1¼ lb) basmati rice

1 tablespoon ghee or salted butter

1 tablespoon cumin seeds

1 large onion, sliced

2–4 bay leaves

8–10 cloves

5 cm (2 in) piece of cinnamon stick

8–10 whole peppercorns

8–10 green cardamom pods, slightly
   opened

800 ml (1½ pints) boiling water

2 tablespoons desiccated coconut

1½ teaspoons salt

½ teaspoon ground turmeric

1 tablespoon roasted cashew nuts,
   chopped

This rice recipe is famous along the western coast of India. It combines a variety of whole spices and is served with both vegetarian and non-vegetarian dishes. The spices will not cause any harm if eaten, but they might be too strong for some tastes. Alternatively, the whole spices can easily be removed from the rice after cooking.

Wash the rice in several changes of water then leave to soak for 10 minutes before draining well.

Heat the ghee or butter in a pan and add the cumin seeds. When they begin to crackle add the sliced onion and sauté until light golden brown. Add the rest of the whole spices and sauté for a further 1–2 minutes over a medium heat.

Reduce the heat and add the drained soaked rice. Using a wooden spoon, fold and turn the rice grains gently until all the grains are moistened and coated with the butter and spiced onion mixture. The grains will start to gradually separate. At this point add the boiling water, coconut, salt and ground turmeric.

Return to the boil. Partially cover the pan and cook for 15 minutes over a medium heat.

Add the cashew nuts, re-cover the pan, reduce the heat and cook for a further 5 minutes. The water should all have been absorbed. Turn off the heat, stir the rice with a wooden spoon and serve hot.

Tip You can easily replace the desiccated coconut with 100 ml (3½ fl oz) canned coconut milk if preferred. Just use 650 ml (22 fl oz) boiling water instead of 800 ml (1½ pints).

FRIED **SWEET POTATOES**

serves four

4 sweet potatoes

1 tablespoon ghee or butter

3 teaspoons sugar

4 scoops vanilla ice cream

½ teaspoon ground cinnamon

This traditional farmers' dessert is easy to make, affordable and absolutely delectable. I love to eat it with vanilla ice cream.

Boil the whole sweet potatoes in their skins for 10–15 minutes or until cooked. Peel and cut into dice.

Heat the ghee or butter in a pan. Add the sugar and reduce the heat. When the sugar begins to caramelize add the diced sweet potatoes and mix well.

Divide the sweet potatoes among 4 serving dishes and serve hot with a scoop of vanilla ice cream sprinkled with ground cinnamon.

COCONUT PANCAKES

serves four

FOR THE PANCAKES

130 g (4¾ oz) all-purpose flour

1 egg

pinch of salt

300 ml (½ pint) milk

1 tablespoon melted butter

FOR THE FILLING

100 g (4 oz) fresh coconut, grated

1 tablespoon sugar

pinch of ground nutmeg or ground
  cardamom or drop of vanilla extract

TO SERVE

honey or maple syrup

vanilla ice cream

Surprise the family with this recipe the next time they ask for sweet pancakes!

To make the pancake batter, mix the all-purpose flour, egg and salt together in a bowl. Pour the milk in slowly and whisk to form a thin batter, ensuring there are no lumps. Thin with a little water if necessary and then mix in the melted butter.

Heat a non-stick 12-cm (5-in) pancake pan. Pour in a little of the batter, about 3 tablespoons, tilting the pan slightly to cover the base completely with the pancake mixture. Cook for about 2 minutes. Turn the pancake over and cook the other side for a further 2 minutes. Remove from the pan and keep warm while you make another 7 pancakes in the same way.

Mix all the pancake filling ingredients together in a bowl. Place each pancake on a plate, one at a time. Spread a spoonful of the mixture down the middle of the pancake and roll up.

Serve the pancakes with either honey or maple syrup and a scoop of vanilla ice cream.

CHAI

serves four

4 teaspoons tea leaves

500 ml (17 fl oz) water

250 ml (8 fl oz) skim or whole milk

4–6 teaspoons sugar (optional)

¼ teaspoon green cardamom pods,
  coarsely crushed in a coffee grinder

½ teaspoon minced ginger

2.5 cm (1 in) piece of cinnamon stick

2–3 cloves garlic, coarsely crushed

6–7 mint leaves

This spiced tea is served in India every time you ask for tea. In India tea is never served by itself, but usually accompanied by fried onion bhajis, Bombay mix or broiled sandwiches.

I have often been asked for this recipe, which I prepare at home every morning. Instead of tea bags I use loose Darjeeling tea leaves, which is messy but worth the effort. Omit the milk if you prefer your tea black but replace it with the same quantity of water.

Combine all the ingredients in a large saucepan. Bring to the boil. Reduce the heat and simmer for 2–3 minutes.

Turn off the heat. Cover and allow to rest for 1 minute.

Strain and serve while still hot.

Opposite: **Coconut pancakes**

A special occasion means so many different things to different people – for some Christmas is the ultimate special day while everyone has different ways of celebrating birthdays and anniversaries. In India there are hundreds of reasons to celebrate, from major Hindu feast days to harvest celebrations – Diwali, the Festival of Lights, is the most widely celebrated festival. I've included some really special dishes in this chapter, from rich meat dishes to saffron-scented desserts and sweets.

special
occasions

LETTUCE ROLLS

serves four

16 iceberg lettuce leaves

15 g (½ oz) butter

½ teaspoon whole cumin seeds

4 tablespoons chopped red bell pepper

50 g (2 oz) mushrooms, finely chopped

1 small onion, finely chopped

1 small carrot, grated

1–2 green chilies, finely chopped

½ teaspoon ground coriander

½ teaspoon salt

½ teaspoon asafetida (optional)

2 tablespoons grated cheese

plain yogurt, Cilantro and Mint Raita
   (see page 13) or sweet mango chutney,
   to serve

This is a great vegetarian starter and is quite a recent innovation in Indian cookery.

Cut each lettuce leaf into a 7.5 x 15 cm (3 x 6 in) rectangle.

Heat the butter in a shallow frying pan and add the cumin seeds. When they begin to crackle add all the vegetables and spices. Cook over a medium heat for 5 minutes. Turn off the heat, sprinkle with the grated cheese and allow to cool.

Blanch the lettuce leaves in boiling water for 45 seconds. Dip in iced water, drain and pat dry with absorbent paper towel.

Divide the cooled vegetable filling mixture into 16 portions and put each portion on a flat lettuce leaf. Fold one long edge of each leaf rectangle towards the middle and then roll up from one short edge to make small "wraps".

Serve the lettuce rolls at room temperature with natural yogurt, Cilantro and Mint Raita or sweet mango chutney.

HOT CHILI SORBET

serves four

250 g (9 oz) green bell peppers, seeded
   and chopped

4–6 green chilies, seeded and chopped

250 ml (8 fl oz) water

2 tablespoons chopped fresh mint

6 teaspoons sugar

½ teaspoon salt

TO GARNISH

unpeeled cucumber slices

sliced red bell pepper

sliced red chilies

Delight your guests by serving this dish between courses.

Place the green bell peppers and chilies in a food processor or blender, add the water and work to a purée.

Transfer the purée to a pan. Add the mint, sugar and salt and bring to the boil. Turn off the heat and leave to cool.

Press the cooled purée mixture through a sieve, pressing hard to push all the purée through the mesh. Pour into small moulds and freeze for about 1 hour.

To serve, dip the bottom of the moulds or ice cube tray into hot water to ease removal of the sorbet from the moulds. Turn the sorbet out on to individual serving dishes, arranging it on top of a slice of cucumber surrounded by long thin slivers of red bell pepper and chili.

GINGERED CRAB

serves four

4 medium to large uncooked crabs

2 tablespoons vegetable oil

2 teaspoons coriander seeds

3 onions, chopped

3 teaspoons minced ginger

3 cloves garlic, crushed

3 green or red chilies, chopped

3 bay leaves

3 teaspoons poppy seeds

2 tablespoons chopped fresh cilantro

300 g (11 oz) canned chopped tomatoes

300 ml (½ pint) canned coconut milk

1 tablespoon garam masala

1½ teaspoons salt

3 tablespoons ground cashew nuts

   (optional)

This is a popular dish from Mumbai, where it is known as adraki kekda. You can use either fresh or frozen crabs – I usually go to the fish market and pick the fleshy or meaty ones. Indian crabs are a greyish-black in colour. Serve hot with rice, pappadums and a raita.

If you are using live crabs, blanch them in boiling water for 2 minutes and allow to cool. Remove all the meat from the shells.

Heat the oil in a deep frying pan and add the coriander seeds. When they begin to crackle and lightly brown add the onions, ginger, garlic, chilies and bay leaves.

Cook for 5–8 minutes over a medium heat before adding the poppy seeds, half the chopped fresh cilantro and the tomatoes. Continue cooking for 10 minutes then add the coconut milk, half the garam masala, the salt and cashew nuts, if using. Cook, uncovered, for a further 5 minutes.

Put the crab flesh in the sauce and cover the pan. Reduce the heat and bring to a simmer. Cook for 25 minutes or until the crab meat is cooked.

Sprinkle with the remaining chopped cilantro and garam masala. Turn off the heat, cover and let stand for 5 minutes before serving.

Tip The sauce can be made 3–4 days in advance and kept in the fridge. Reheat it thoroughly before adding the crab meat.

PRAWN BALICHOW

serves four

6–8 cloves

2.5 cm (1 in) piece of cinnamon stick

1½ teaspoons black mustard seeds

4 tablespoons vegetable oil

1 kg (2¼ lb) raw prawns (thawed weight
   if frozen), peeled and deveined

2 large onions, chopped

2 large tomatoes, chopped

250 ml (8 fl oz) malt vinegar

2 teaspoons minced ginger

4 teaspoons minced garlic

1½ teaspoons ground cumin

6–8 chopped hot red chilies

2 tablespoons brown sugar

1½ teaspoons salt

*Originally called prawn balcho, this was a main dish that has
now become a relish or pickle, best served with flaky parathas
(see page 12).*

Grind the cloves, cinnamon and mustard seeds coarsely in a
coffee grinder.

Heat the oil in a pan and fry the prawns for 2–3 minutes.
Remove the prawns from the oil using a slotted spoon and
leave to drain on absorbent paper towels. Cook the onions in
the same oil until translucent, about 5–8 minutes.

Add the tomatoes and cook for 8–10 minutes. Add the
vinegar, ginger, garlic, ground cumin, red chilies and the ground
cloves mixture. Stir and cook, uncovered, for 10 minutes.

Return the fried prawns to the pan, together with the sugar
and salt. Cook for 5–8 minutes until the sauce has reduced to a
thick gravy consistency.

SCALLOPS COOKED WITH **MILD GOAN SPICES**

serves four

20 g (¾ oz) butter

3 shallots or small red onions, finely diced

2 x 2.5 cm (1 in) pieces of cinnamon stick

6 cloves

5 green onions, finely chopped

1 chili, finely diced (optional)

100 ml (3½ fl oz) dry white wine

½ teaspoon salt

½ teaspoon freshly cracked black pepper

1 tablespoon whipping cream

675 g (1½ lb) scallops

200 ml (7 fl oz) water

2 teaspoons lemon juice

pinch of ground nutmeg

1 teaspoon chopped fresh cilantro
  (optional)

The state of Goa on the west coast of India is famous for its seafood dishes. I first ate this delicately spiced dish from the northern beach huts in Goa and it has now become a firm favourite when I am cooking for a special occasion.

Heat the butter in a pan and cook the shallots or red onions for 3–4 minutes. Add the cinnamon, cloves, green onions and chili. Add the wine, cover and cook for 10–12 minutes. Add the salt, pepper and cream.

Place the scallops in a separate pan and add the water and lemon juice. Simmer gently for 10 minutes. Pour the spiced onion and wine sauce, which should be fairly thick, onto a plate and add the drained scallops. Season to taste. Sprinkle with ground nutmeg and chopped fresh cilantro, if using, and serve.

SOUR FISH CURRY

1 kg (2¼ lb) cod, thinly sliced

1 teaspoon ground turmeric

1 teaspoon salt

1 tablespoon coriander seeds

1 tablespoon cumin seeds

6 dried red chilies

6 cloves

2.5 cm (1 in) piece of cinnamon stick

2 tablespoons vegetable oil

2 onions, finely chopped

4 tablespoons desiccated coconut

1 tablespoon minced ginger

1 tablespoon minced garlic

1 tablespoon vinegar

300 ml (½ pint) water

2 tablespoons tamarind pulp

A Goan dish, this curry was originally introduced by the Portuguese to India with fewer spices than today's typical recipe. Serve the curry hot with plain steamed or boiled rice.

Marinate the fish slices by rubbing ground turmeric and salt over them. Set aside for 20 minutes.

Dry-fry the coriander and cumin seeds, dried red chilies, cloves and cinnamon in a frying pan for 2–3 minutes. Put the spices in a coffee grinder and grind to a coarse blend.

Heat the oil in a pan. Add the onions and sauté until golden brown. Add the desiccated coconut, ground spice blend, ginger and garlic to the pan and cook for 2 minutes or until the coconut begins to brown.

Add the vinegar and the water and bring to the boil. Lower the fish slices into the sauce and cook for 5–7 minutes.

Stir in the tamarind pulp. Adjust the seasoning to taste and serve hot.

CHICKEN WITH SPINACH AND FENUGREEK

serves four

1½ tablespoons vegetable oil

200 g (7 oz) tomatoes, chopped

100 ml (3½ fl oz) water

50 g (2 oz) cashew nuts

1 teaspoon dried fenugreek leaves

1 teaspoon ground cardamom

1½ teaspoons sugar

salt

350 g (12 oz) chicken, cut into 2.5–4 cm
   (1–1½ in) cubes

75 g (3 oz) whole baby spinach leaves

75 ml (3 fl oz) light cream

This dish uses spinach leaves but watercress can be also be used.

Place the oil, chopped tomatoes, water and cashew nuts in a pan and cook over a medium heat for 15-20 minutes. Blend in a food processor to a fine purée.

Return to the pan and reheat. Add the fenugreek leaves and ground cardamom, followed by the sugar and a little salt to taste. Stir in the chicken pieces and cook for 15 minutes over a medium heat, stirring occasionally.

Add the spinach leaves and cook for 3–4 minutes. Stir in the cream and serve garnished with "streaks" of light cream.

Opposite: **Chicken with spinach and fenugreek**

CHICKEN IN CARDAMOM CREAM SAUCE

serves four

2 tablespoons vegetable oil

1 teaspoon cumin seeds

2 cloves

3 green cardamom pods

2 bay leaves

2 medium onions, chopped

2 teaspoons ground coriander

2 tomatoes, chopped

350 g (12 oz) chicken, cut into 2.5–4 cm
(1–1½ in) cubes

100 ml (3½ fl oz) light cream

2 teaspoons ground cardamom

½ teaspoon dried fenugreek leaves

1 teaspoon garam masala

½ teaspoon sugar

salt

Green cardamoms grow on small bushes, whose stems spread themselves on the ground from which the pods grow. Whenever I am in south India on a visit to the plantations in the famous Cardamom Hills, I like to get fresh cardamoms which haven't yet been dried for consumer use. This recipe, however, uses dried cardamoms, which is their most widely available form.

Heat the oil in a pan and add the cumin seeds, cloves, cardamom pods and bay leaves. When they begin to crackle add the chopped onions and fry for 5–10 minutes over a medium heat.

Add the ground coriander and chopped tomatoes and fry for another 2 minutes.

Add the diced chicken and fry, stirring continuously, for about 5 minutes.

Add the light cream, ground cardamom, fenugreek leaves and garam masala. Bring to the boil and simmer for 10–15 minutes. Add the sugar and salt to taste. Serve hot.

Tip Instead of using ready ground cardamom, you may wish to grind whole green cardamom pods yourself. Crush the pods with a mortar and pestle to crack the outer shells. The black seeds inside are the spice so remove the cracked pods before grinding the seeds.

AROMATIC SPICED LAMB

serves four

2 tablespoons vegetable oil

½ teaspoon mustard oil

2 onions, sliced

1 tablespoon minced garlic

1 teaspoon minced ginger

1 teaspoon ground cardamom

675 g (1½ lb) boned lamb, cut into 2.5–4 cm
   (1–1½ in) cubes

1 teaspoon ground coriander

1 teaspoon ground cumin

¼ teaspoon ground nutmeg

¼ teaspoon ground cinnamon

4 tablespoons plain yogurt

1 teaspoon ground black pepper

1½ teaspoons salt

1 teaspoon sliced fresh ginger, to garnish

This is an authentic Hyderabadi dish eaten at festive occasions.

Heat the vegetable and mustard oils in a large, heavy-bottomed pan. Add the sliced onions and cook over a moderate heat for about 10–15 minutes or until the onions are dark brown.

Add the garlic, ginger and ground cardamom. Cook, stirring, for 2–3 minutes. Add the lamb and all the other ingredients. Cover with a tight lid and cook until the lamb is cooked – about 30 minutes. Add a little water if the meat begins to stick to the pan.

Serve hot, garnished with sliced ginger.

LAMB IN A CREAMY SAUCE

serves four

100 g (4 oz) cashew nuts

2 tablespoons vegetable oil

1 teaspoon cumin seeds

2 cloves

2 bay leaves

2 green cardamom pods

1 large onion, sliced

3 teaspoons minced garlic

1 teaspoon ground turmeric

½ teaspoon chili powder

1 teaspoon garam masala

2 teaspoons ground coriander

350 g (12 oz) boned lamb, cut into 2.5–4 cm
   (1–1½ in) cubes

100 ml (3½ fl oz) light cream

salt

1 tablespoon chopped fresh cilantro, to
   garnish

This creamy lamb curry is cooked at festive occasions. The ground cashew nuts help give it a deliciously rich consistency. As an alternative garnish, sprinkle with toasted almond slivers.

Soak the cashew nuts in hot water for 2–3 hours then drain and grind to a fine paste. Set aside.

Heat the oil in a pan. Add the cumin seeds, cloves, bay leaves and cardamom pods. When they begin to crackle, add the sliced onions and fry for about 5–10 minutes over a medium heat.

Add the minced garlic, ground turmeric, chili powder, garam masala and ground coriander. Sprinkle with a little water and continue to cook for 2–3 minutes.

Add the cubed lamb and sauté for 5 minutes to seal the meat on all sides.

Add the cashew nut paste and mix well. Add a little water if the mixture becomes too thick and continue to cook for 20–25 minutes, covered, over a low heat.

Remove the lid, add the light cream to the curry and add salt to taste. Cook, uncovered, for 5 minutes to dry off any excess moisture.

Serve garnished with fresh cilantro.

Tip Toasted almond slivers make an attractive garnish. Simply heat a cast-iron frying pan until hot and add the almond slivers. Toss the almonds for a few minutes in the hot pan, making sure they do not burn.

SMOKED LAMB
WITH **SAFFRON**

serves four

4 tablespoons milk

8–10 saffron strands

1 tablespoon vegetable oil

675 g (1½ lb) lamb, cut into 2.5–4 cm
**   (1–1½ in) cubes**

2 onions, chopped

2 cloves garlic, chopped

100 ml (3½ fl oz) water

½ teaspoon salt

2 teaspoons paprika

1 red bell pepper, cut into strips

2 tomatoes, diced

2–3 green chilies

Simple, easy and delicious, this dish comes from the southern city of Hyderabad. I sometimes make it with chicken or pork instead of lamb. Serve it with cumin rice (see page 13) or naan bread.

Heat the milk and soak the saffron strands in the hot liquid.

Meanwhile, heat the oil in a pan and sear the meat until browned all over. Remove the meat from the oil and set aside.

Sauté the onions in the same oil until translucent. Add the garlic and cook for 1–2 minutes. Return the seared meat to the pan. Add the water, cover and cook for 25–30 minutes or until the lamb is cooked.

Add the salt, paprika, red bell pepper and diced tomatoes. Continue cooking, covered, for 5 minutes over a medium heat.

Meanwhile, dry-fry the green chilies in a frying pan until the outside skin starts to blacken in spots. Reduce the heat and continue tossing the chilies in the pan until all the green skin has turned blackish-brown. Remove the chilies from the pan and grind them in a coffee grinder or coarsely crush or chop.

Add the saffron and milk to the meat and bring to the boil. Turn off the heat. Sprinkle the smoked chili onto the meat. Cover and let it stand for 5 minutes, before serving.

POTATOES AND GREEN BELL PEPPERS COOKED WITH PEANUTS AND COCONUT

2 tablespoons vegetable oil

½ teaspoon cumin seeds

1½ teaspoons minced ginger

1 green chili, chopped

1 green bell pepper, seeded and diced

250 g (9 oz) boiled potatoes, diced

75 g (3 oz) crushed peanuts

1 teaspoon sugar

1 teaspoon ground cumin

juice of ½ lemon

salt

25 g (1 oz) desiccated coconut or grated
   fresh coconut

2 tablespoons chopped fresh cilantro

This potato, peanut and coconut dish is commonly eaten by the farmers of Maharashtra. I've given it a new twist by adding green bell peppers.

Heat the oil in a pan and add the cumin seeds. When they begin to crackle add the ginger and green chili and reduce the heat. Add the diced green bell pepper and continue to fry over a low heat.

After 2–3 minutes stir in the boiled potatoes, then the crushed peanuts. Add the sugar, ground cumin, lemon juice and salt to taste and mix well.

Serve sprinkled with grated coconut and chopped fresh cilantro.

MINT AND
POTATO PULAV

serves four

250 g (9 oz) basmati rice

3 tablespoons mint leaves, plus extra
   to garnish

3 cloves garlic

1 cm (½ in) piece of fresh ginger

1 green chili

1 tablespoon chopped fresh cilantro

4 tablespoons vegetable oil

3 cloves

3 green cardamom pods

3 bay leaves

½ teaspoon cumin seeds

1 onion, chopped

2 potatoes, peeled and diced

salt

Mint is not the most commonly used herb in Indian dishes but this fresh tasting mint and rice dish from the southern state of Hyderabad is wonderful served with a lamb curry like Smoked Lamb with Saffron (see page 112).

Wash the rice in several changes of water then leave to soak for 10 minutes before draining well.

Combine the mint leaves, garlic, ginger, chili and fresh cilantro in a blender and work to a fine paste. Add a little water if required.

Heat the oil in a pan then add the cloves, cardamom pods, bay leaves and cumin seeds. When they begin to crackle add the chopped onion and fry over a medium heat.

When the onions begin to soften, add the potatoes, drained soaked rice and mint paste mixture. Stir gently. Add enough hot water to come to a level 1 cm (¹/₂ in) above the layer of rice. Add salt as required and bring to the boil.

Once the water begins to boil, reduce the heat to a simmer. Cover with a lid and leave to cook. After about 15–20 minutes, remove the lid and check whether the rice is cooked. Stir once gently to avoid the rice breaking up. Replace the lid and turn off the heat.

After about 5 minutes transfer the pulav to a serving bowl. Serve hot, garnished with a few mint leaves, and with a fresh raita as an accompaniment (see pages 13–14).

SMOKED PURÉED EGGPLANTS WITH SPICES

serves four

3 large eggplants

2 tablespoons vegetable oil

½ teaspoon cumin seeds

2.5 cm (1 in) piece of fresh ginger, chopped

1 green chili, chopped

1 large onion, chopped

2 teaspoons minced garlic

½ teaspoon ground turmeric

½ teaspoon chili powder

1 teaspoon ground coriander

250 g (9 oz) tomatoes, chopped

1 teaspoon ground cumin

salt

1 tablespoon chopped fresh cilantro, to garnish

I absolutely adore eggplants – they are one of my favourite vegetables which is why I like to prepare this dish for special family occasions. It is great as an accompaniment but sometimes I also combine it with yogurt and serve it as a dip with plain pappadums.

Preheat the oven to 240°C (475°F), Gas 9.

Rub the skins of the eggplants with 1 tablespoon of the oil. Place them on a baking tray and cook in the oven for 15–20 minutes until the outer skin becomes burnt and the inner flesh is soft. Remove the skins when cool enough to handle and put the flesh in a bowl.

Heat the remaining oil in a pan and add the cumin seeds. When they begin to crackle add the chopped ginger and green chili. After 1 minute add the chopped onions and fry for 4–5 minutes.

Stir in the minced garlic and continue to fry. Add the ground turmeric, chili powder and ground coriander. Sprinkle with water and fry for another minute.

Add the chopped tomatoes and continue to cook over a medium heat for 5–8 minutes.

Place the eggplant pulp on a chopping board and chop with a large knife, then stir into the spicy "masala". Add the ground cumin and salt to taste, sprinkle with chopped fresh cilantro and serve.

Tip For an alternative dip, try replacing the eggplant pulp with an equal quantity of mashed potato.

FENUGREEK-FLAVOURED
DEEP-FRIED **BREAD**

serves four

75 g (3 oz) fresh fenugreek leaves

salt

250 g (9 oz) wholewheat flour

½ teaspoon ground turmeric

½ teaspoon cumin seeds

1 teaspoon ground cumin

½ teaspoon chili powder

1 tablespoon chopped fresh cilantro

1 tablespoon oil, plus extra for deep-frying

plain yogurt, to serve

This deep-fried bread, methi puri, comes from western Gujarat and is commonly eaten with plain yogurt. It uses fresh fenugreek leaves, which are available by the bunch in most Indian food stores. Pick the leaves from the stalk and wash them before use. Freeze any leaves left after making this recipe by drying them well on absorbent paper towels and freezing them in an airtight container.

Chop the fenugreek leaves, sprinkle with salt and rub in well. Leave for about 5–10 minutes then squeeze the fenugreek leaves to remove excess juices and put in a bowl.

Add the flour to the bowl together with the ground turmeric, cumin seeds, ground cumin, chili powder, chopped fresh cilantro and a little salt.

Sprinkle in enough water to make a stiff dough. Add 1 tablespoon of oil and knead well using your hands. Set aside for 30 minutes.

Divide the dough into 16. Roll out each piece on a floured board into a flat round of 7.5–10 cm (3–4 in) diameter.

Heat the oil for deep-frying in a deep pan to 180°C (350°F) then fry each puri, one at a time, for about 45–60 seconds until golden brown. Remove from the pan with a slotted spoon and drain on absorbent paper towels.

Serve immediately with plain yogurt.

SAFFRON SEMOLINA PUDDING

1½ teaspoons ghee

10–15 raisins

10–15 cashew nuts, roughly chopped

150 g (5 oz) semolina

75 g (3 oz) sugar

300 ml (½ pint) milk

pinch of saffron strands

slivers of almonds, to decorate (optional)

Saffron is considered the world's most expensive spice: gifts of saffron are exchanged at Diwali, the Hindu Festival of Lights and this is traditionally a dessert made on festive occasions. However, if, like me, you have a sweet tooth, you will find that you don't need an excuse to prepare this delicious dessert.

Heat the ghee in a pan and add the raisins and chopped cashew nuts. After about 2 minutes add the semolina, reduce the heat and cook, stirring, for 2–3 minutes.

Add the sugar and mix well. Pour in the milk and add the saffron. Cook over a low to medium heat, whisking well.

When the mixture begins to thicken and the semolina is cooked remove from the heat. Decorate with slivers of almonds, if desired, and serve hot.

SAFFRON-FLAVOURED
THICK YOGURT

serves four

500 g (1¼ lb) plain yogurt

100 g (4 oz) sugar

pinch saffron strands

100 ml (3½ fl oz) milk

Better than fruit yogurt, this dessert is commonly made during the summer months in India to counteract the scorching summer heat.

Tip the plain yogurt onto a piece of cheesecloth. Bring together the 4 corners of the cloth, tie them into a knot and hang the cloth of yogurt over a bowl or sink to let the excess water from the yogurt drain away. Leave overnight.

The next day tip the drained thick yogurt into a bowl and whisk in the sugar until it dissolves.

Heat the saffron and milk together in a pan and cook over a low heat for 10–15 minutes until the milk reduces and becomes dark yellow in colour. Whisk the milk into the yogurt.

Pour the yogurt mixture into 4 serving dishes. Refrigerate when cool and serve chilled.

Opposite: **Saffron semolina pudding**

NUTTY BARFI

**100 g (4 oz) cashew nuts, coarsely ground,
  or ready chopped cashew nuts (very
  small pieces)**

**100 g (4 oz) shelled pistachios, coarsely
  ground**

100 g (4 oz) almonds, coarsely ground

50 g (2 oz) desiccated coconut

2 teaspoons ground green cardamom

1 teaspoon ground nutmeg

300 g (11 oz) sugar

175 ml (6 fl oz) water

**8–10 saffron strands steeped in 1 teaspoon
  hot water**

200 g (7 oz) ghee

75 g (3 oz) coarse semolina

100 g (4 oz) chickpea flour (besan)

TO DECORATE (OPTIONAL)

slivers of pistachios

slivers of almonds

saffron strands

I usually grind the nuts for this recipe in a coffee grinder. This barfi keeps well at room temperature for 7 days. In a warmer climate keep it in the fridge and simply heat for 30 seconds in a microwave before serving.

Mix all the chopped nuts, desiccated coconut, ground cardamom and nutmeg in a large bowl.

Combine the sugar and water in a pan and heat until the sugar melts. Reduce the heat and simmer for 5–8 minutes. Add the saffron together with the steeping water.

Meanwhile, heat the ghee in a wok. When it becomes very hot and melts, reduce the heat and add the semolina. Cook, stirring continuously. After 10 minutes or when the semolina turns golden brown, add the chickpea flour. Cook for 5 minutes, stirring continuously. Stir this mixture into the nuts, mixing well with a wooden spoon, then add the sugar syrup.

Pour the mixture while hot into a baking tray. Leave to cool. Decorate the barfi with slivers of pistachios, almonds and strands of saffron if desired. Cut into squares and serve.

PISTACHIO AND COCONUT BARFI

serves four

4 tablespoons melted ghee

300 ml (½ pint) canned coconut milk

150 g (5 oz) milk powder

150 g (5 oz) desiccated coconut

4 tablespoons water

150 g (5 oz) sugar

2 teaspoons ground cardamom

6 tablespoons shelled chopped green
   pistachios

½ teaspoon ground nutmeg

saffron stands, to decorate (optional)

Like the Nutty Barfi opposite, this dessert is often made for special occasions and always during Diwali.

Lightly grease a 25–28 cm (10–11 in) baking tray with 1 teaspoon of the ghee. Heat the remaining ghee in a saucepan. Add the coconut milk and stir in the milk powder, ensuring there are no lumps in the mixture. Add the desiccated coconut, water, sugar, ground cardamom, pistachios and nutmeg and mix well. The mixture should be fairly thick.

Reduce the heat and continue to cook, stirring, for 5–7 minutes. Remove from the heat and empty the contents of the pan into the baking tray. Spread out the mixture and flatten it evenly. Smooth the top, sprinkle over a few strands of saffron, if using, and refrigerate for 4–5 hours.

Cut the barfi into squares, arrange on a serving dish and serve chilled or at room temperature.

GLOSSARY OF INGREDIENTS

The following herbs and spices are referred to in many of the recipes in this book. Some of them may be more familiar than others and the majority are easily found in large supermarkets. Others may need to be purchased from a specialist food shop or Asian grocer. Indian names are in brackets.

Ajowan (ajwain)
Ajowan seeds look very similar to cumin seeds and have a strong, distinctive flavour that resembles aniseed. The spice is used to add a zing to many fish and vegetable dishes as well as some Indian breads. The seeds are often chewed on their own to alleviate stomach pains.

Asafetida (hing)
Asafetida has a very overpowering, almost unpleasant smell, which is calmed when it is fried in oil. Asafetida is made from a dried gum resin which is ground to a yellowish powder which is used in small quantities in cooking in many lentil and vegetable dishes.

Cardamom (elaichi)
Cardamom has a delicate, aromatic fragrance, which is used to flavour meat and vegetable dishes as well as desserts and drinks. It is an essential ingredient in garam masala (see page 11). You will see brown cardamom pods as well as the pale green ones but the green ones have a much finer flavour.

Chat masala
This spice mix, made with salt, pepper, cumin seeds, ground ginger and dried mango, is available ready-mixed from Asian grocers.

Chilies, dried (lal mirch)
There are a confusing number of chili varieties but the most commonly used dried chilies in Indian cooking are the small, red ones – they will add a fiery heat to any dish. They can be used whole, crushed, flaked or in powdered form. Remove the seeds before using to lessen the heat, if you wish.

Chilies, fresh (hari mirch)
I generally use the long thin green chilies when fresh ones are called for, although they can vary in heat so use with caution. The seeds can be removed to make them less fiery. Always wash your hands after handling chilies.

Cilantro, fresh (hara dhaniya)
Fresh green cilantro is used as a herb and has a lovely fresh fragrance. It is used to make chutneys and dips and makes a wonderful garnish.

Cinnamon (dalchini)
The spice used in cooking is the dried inner bark of the cinnamon tree. It is one of the earliest known spices and is an essential ingredient of garam masala. It is used in its "stick" form as well as a ground spice and its warm, sweet aroma enhances rice dishes, as well as meat dishes and desserts. In Ayurvedic medicine, it is used to alleviate headaches, colds and rheumatic pains.

Cloves (long)
Cloves are the small, dried buds of the clove tree, which have a sweet aroma but a bitter taste. They are used to flavour rice and savoury dishes and are also used in spice mixtures, such as garam masala.

Coriander seeds (dhaniya)

The pungent, slightly sweet, citrus flavour of coriander seeds is used in vegetable, meat, fish and poultry dishes. The seeds come from a leafy herb bearing lacy flowers – these seeds are dried and used extensively, whole or ground, as an aromatic spice in Indian cooking. The whole seeds are often dry-roasted and then coarsely crushed with other spices to make a spice mixture. The flavour of the ground spice is not as intense as that of whole seeds.

Cumin (jeera)

The distinctive aroma of cumin seeds is used to flavour rice and curries. Cumin seeds are the fruits of a small annual herb, which grows throughout India. They are used dried and range in colour from light, greenish brown to dark brown. They can be fried in hot oil to intensify their flavour or dry-roasted and then ground with other spices. Ready-ground cumin is available from super-markets but it quickly loses its flavour. Another variety of cumin is black cumin (kala jeera), although black cumin is less aromatic and not as bitter in flavour.

Curry leaves (kari patta)

This aromatic herb is used to add flavour to many dishes, particularly in southern India, but it also has medicinal properties and can ease stomach pains. Despite its name, it has no flavour of curry and is actually related to the lemon family. Curry leaves are fried in hot oil which brings out their nutty flavour. I often freeze curry leaves; first wash them and then leave to dry on tea towels. Then simply put them into a bag and place in the freezer.

Fennel seeds (saunf)

Dried fennel seeds are used throughout India, not only to add a sweet, aniseed flavour to a variety of dishes, but also as a mouth freshener. They are similar in appearance to cumin seeds though greener in colour.

Fenugreek (methi)

Fenugreek is used to flavour a variety of dishes and is also used in bread making (see page 117). It is one of the most powerful and ancient spices, believed to aid digestion. Its leaves are used both fresh and dried and the dried seeds are commonly used in ground spice mixes. Dried fenugreek leaves are often referred to as kasoori methi.

Ghee

Ghee is clarified butter that can be used for deep-frying without burning – it has a delicious buttery taste, although vegetable oil can be substituted in most cases. You can buy it in all Indian grocers.

Ginger (adrak)

Ginger has a pungent, fresh aroma and has been prescribed for many ailments – a ginger infusion is great for a sore throat or cold, as well as travel sickness and nausea. It is the underground root or rhizome of a herbaceous plant grown throughout Asia. In its fresh state it is most often used as a pulp to add a distinctive flavour to a variety of dishes. Dried ginger is also available as a ground spice which can be used to flavour drinks as well as savoury and sweet dishes.

Mustard seeds (rai)

Mustard seeds are used to flavour a variety of dishes, particularly those from Bengal. Whole black mustard seeds are often thrown into hot oil or "popped" at the beginning of a recipe – this gives them a sweet, nutty taste that enhances vegetables, legumes and fish dishes. There are three types of mustard seeds, of which brown and black are the most widely used in India.

Nutmeg (jaiphal)

Nutmeg has a warm, sweet flavour and is used in small quantities in desserts, often grated from a whole nutmeg. It is also used in some garam masala mixes. Nutmeg is believed to help overcome bronchitis and rheumatism.

Pepper (kalimiri)

Pepper is the most commonly used spice and is sometimes known as the King of Spices. It is the fruit of a perennial vine which bears berries or peppercorns. The black, white, red and green varieties all come from the same plant – the difference in colour occurs in the way they are processed. Black pepper is made by drying green peppercorns in the sun while white pepper is made when ripe berries are softened in water, hulled and then dried.

Saffron (kesar)

Saffron is considered the most expensive spice in the world and is worth its weight in gold. It is actually made from the stigmas of the crocus flower, which are hand picked and dried in the sun. A gift of saffron is something very special and it is often exchanged at Diwali. Saffron, which is sold as strands and as a powder, is used in very small quantities to flavour both savoury and sweet dishes, particularly for special occasions.

Tamarind (imli)

The tamarind tree is evergreen and bears long, crescent-shaped pods. Within these pods are the seeds, surrounded by a fleshy pulp. It is this pulp, with its fruity sweet-and-sour aroma, that is used in Indian cooking. According to Ayurvedic medicine, it is beneficial as a mild laxative, and tamarind water is often recommended to soothe a sore throat.

Turmeric (haldi)

Although used mainly for colour, this spice imparts a subtle flavour and is also used extensively for its antiseptic and digestive properties. This bright yellow, bitter-tasting spice is sold ground although the small roots are also available fresh or dried. Like ginger, it needs to be peeled and ground before using. If your hands become stained when preparing fresh turmeric, you can clean them by rubbing them with potato peelings.

INDEX

Amritsar fish curry 34
aromatic spiced lamb 109

baby corn and crunchy green beans 45
baby corn and mushrooms in a spicy
    tomato and onion sauce 69
baked garlic and chili cheese oysters 58
barfi, nutty 120
barfi, pistachio and coconut 121
beans and legumes:
    garlic-flavoured lentils 44
    Gujarati dal 95
    kitcheri 95
    spiced beans on naan bread 21
    spiced kidney beans with ginger and
        yogurt 66
beansprout and peanut salad 51
beet pudding 74
blackened spiced cod 83
Bombay mixed vegetable sandwich 24
breads:
    chapatti 11
    fenugreek-flavoured deep-fried bread
        117
    flaky flat bread with a spiced egg
        coating 32
    paratha 12
    spiced deep-fried puris 72
    spinach and chickpea flour bread 73

cabbage, dry spiced 92
carrot pudding, Indian 52
chai 98
chapatti 11
cheese-stuffed peppers 22
chicken:
    chicken in almond sauce 62
    chicken in cardamom cream sauce 108
    chicken with green onions 86
    chicken with green peppers 25
    chicken with peanuts 40
    chicken with spinach and fenugreek
        106

chicken in a strong garlic sauce 59
chicken stuffed with cashew nuts,
    cheese and peas 61
dry spiced chicken 38
easy grilled chicken bites 80
slow-cooked chicken with baby onions 88
spiced chicken in a tomato and mint
    sauce 85
chickpea flour bread, spinach and 73
chickpea flour pancakes 78
chili sorbet, hot 102
chutney, date and lime 14
cilantro and mint raita 13
coconut pancakes 98
cod, blackened spiced 83
cool mango soup 75
couscous salad, spicy 49
crab, gingered 103
crispy coconut prawns with tangy mango
    sauce 37
cumin rice 13

dal, Gujarati 95
date and lime chutney 14
deep-fried spiced new potatoes 43
desserts:
    beet pudding 74
    coconut pancakes 98
    fried sweet potatoes 97
    Indian carrot pudding 52
    nutty barfi 120
    pistachio and coconut barfi 121
    saffron-flavoured thick yogurt 119
    saffron semolina pudding 119
    tangy fruit salad 29
devilled prawns 80
drinks:
    chai 98
    iced lime water 15
    lassi 15
dry spiced cabbage 92
dry spiced chicken 38

easy grilled chicken bites 80
eggplant dip 18
eggplant, tangy circles of 50
eggplants and potatoes 70
eggplants, smoked puréed 116
eggs:
    flaky flat bread with a spicy egg
        coating 32

spicy French toast 18
spicy scrambled eggs 43
spicy spinach with eggs 28

fennel and green bean vermicelli,
    steamed 47
fenugreek-flavoured deep-fried bread
    117
fish and seafood:
    Amritsar fish curry 34
    baked garlic and chili cheese oysters
        58
    blackened spiced cod 83
    crispy coconut prawns with tangy
        mango sauce 37
    devilled prawns 80
    fish in fennel and cream 56
    fish in a tangy minty sauce 37
    gingered crab 103
    Indian fried fish 84
    monkfish with mushrooms 56
    mustard fish curry 33
    prawn balichow 104
    prawns with spinach 57
    prawns in sweet lime curry with
        mandarin oranges 58
    scallops cooked with mild Goan spices
        105
    sour fish curry 106
    spiced fried fish 24
flaky flat bread with a spiced egg coating
    32
French toast, spicy 18
fried sweet potatoes 97
fruit salad, tangy 28

garam masala 11
garlic-flavoured lentils 44
garlic, minced, to prepare 9
ginger, minced, to prepare 9
gingered crab 103
gingered potatoes and onions 42
gingery turnips 27
Goan rice 96
gravy, spiced 15
green peppers, chicken with 25
green bell peppers, potatoes and 114
ground meat with spinach, spiced 41
Gujarati dal 95

herbs 10
hot chili sorbet 102

iced lime water 15
Indian carrot pudding 52
Indian fried fish 84

kitcheri 95

lamb:
    aromatic spiced lamb 109
    lamb in a cashew nut and mint sauce 91
    lamb in a creamy sauce 111
    lamb and potato curry 67
    rice with ground lamb 89
    smoked lamb with saffron 112
    spiced ground lamb balls 20
    spiced ground meat with spinach 41
    lamb's liver baked with fennel 66
lassi 15
lentils, garlic-flavoured 44
lettuce rolls 102

mango soup, cool 75
masala pappadums 22
Meena Pathak's pumpkin soup 79
menu planning 8
mint and potato pulav 115
mixed vegetable raita 14
monkfish with mushrooms 56
mustard fish curry 33

nutty barfi 120

okra with onions 27
okra stuffed with spices, whole 44
okra in yogurt 92
onions, to prepare 9
oysters, baked garlic and chili cheese 58

pancakes, chickpea flour 78
pancakes, coconut 98
pappadums, masala 22
paratha 12
pasta with curry sauce 21
peppers, cheese-stuffed 22
pineapple relish, spiced 14
pistachio and coconut barfi 121
pork with pickling spices 65
potatoes:
    eggplants and potatoes 70

deep-fried spiced new potatoes 43
gingered potatoes and onions 42
    mint and potato pulav 115
    potatoes and green bell peppers
      cooked with peanuts and coconut 114
prawn balichow 104
prawns, crispy coconut 37
prawns, devilled 80
pulav, mint and potato 115
pumpkin soup, Meena Pathak's 79
puris, spinach deep-fried 72

raita, cilantro and mint 13
raita, mixed vegetable 14
relish, spiced pineapple 14
rice, cumin 13
rice, Goan 96
rice with ground lamb 89
rice, perfect basmati 12
rice, spiced 49
rice, tamarind 70

saffron-flavoured thick yogurt 119
saffron semolina pudding 119
salad, beansprout and peanut 51
salad, spicy couscous 49
sandwich, Bombay mixed vegetable 24
scallops cooked with mild Goan spiced
    105
semolina pudding, saffron 119
slow-cooked chicken with baby onions
    88
smoked lamb with saffron 112
smoked puréed eggplants with spices
    116
sorbet, hot chili 102
soup, cool mango 754
soup, Meena Pathak's pumpkin 79
sour fish curry 106
spiced beans on naan bread 21
spiced chicken in a tomato and mint
    sauce 85
spiced deep-fried puris 72
spiced fried fish 24
spiced gravy 15
spiced ground lamb balls 20
spiced kidney beans with ginger and
    yogurt 66
spiced pineapple relish 14
spiced rice 49
spices 10

spicy couscous salad 49
spicy French toast 18
spicy scrambled eggs 43
spicy spinach with eggs 28
spinach with caramelized onions and
    sultanas 46
spinach and chickpea flour bread 73
spinach with eggs, spicy 28
steamed fennel and green bean
    vermicelli 47
sweet potatoes, fried 97

tamarind rice 70
tandoori grilled vegetables 81
tangy circles of eggplant 50
tangy fruit salad 28
turnips, gingery 27

vegetables:
    baby corn and crunchy green beans
      45
    baby corn and mushrooms in a spicy
      tomato and onion sauce 69
    Bombay mixed vegetable sandwich 24
    cheese-stuffed peppers 22
    dry spiced cabbage 92
    eggplants with potatoes 70
    gingery turnips 27
    hot chili sorbet 102
    lettuce rolls 102
    mixed vegetable raita 14
    okra with onions 27
    okra in yogurt 92
    smoked puréed eggplants with spices
      116
    spinach with caramelized onions and
      sultanas 46
    steamed fennel and green bean
      vermicelli 47
    tandoori grilled vegetables 81
    tangy circles of eggplant 56
    vermicelli, steamed fennel and green
      bean 47
    whole okra stuffed with spices 44

whole okra stuffed with spices 44

yogurt, saffron-flavoured thick

USEFUL ADDRESSES

Many Indian ingredients are now readily available in supermarkets. For more unusual ingredients, fresh produce or for fresh whole spices, you should head to an Indian grocery store.

Some areas of the country, especially urban centres like Toronto and Vancouver, have a large Indian community and this is where you will find the greatest concentration of specialist shops. At the Punjabi Market in Vancouver (centring around the junction of Main Street and 49th Avenue) you will be able to find every ingredient imaginable. In Toronto you can find the area known as "Little India" along Gerrard Street East, where a large selection of specialty shops provide all the ingredients you need to make authentic Indian cuisine.

The following is a small (and by no means comprehensive) list of stores that carry the ingredients in this book.

ALBERTA

The Cookbook Company Cooks
722 - 11th Ave. S.W. Calgary, AB
(403) 265-6066 or 1-800-663-8532

India Bazaar
4514 - 118 Avenue
Edmonton, AB
(403) 539-5100

Millwoods Spice Centre
3930 – 91 Street
Edmonton, AB
(403) 463-5877

Spice Bazaar
9236 – 34 Avenue NW
Edmonton, AB
(403) 988-5684

Spice Centre
9217 – 34 Avenue
Edmonton, AB
(403) 461-5724

BRITISH COLUMBIA

All India Foods
6517 Main Street
Vancouver, BC
(604) 324-2195

The Gourmet Warehouse
1856 Pandora Street (off alley)
Vancouver, BC
(604) 253-3022

India Bazaar
9278 – 120th Street
Surrey, BC
(604) 583-9278

The Pepper Pot
Lonsdale Quay Market
North Vancouver, BC
(604) 986-1877

Singh Foods
6684 Main Street
Vancouver, BC
(604) 327-4911

The South China Seas Trading Company
Granville Island Public Market
Vancouver, BC
(604) 681-5402

MANITOBA

Dino's Grocery Mart
460 Notre Dame Avenue
Winnipeg, MB
(204) 942-1526

ONTARIO

Asian Grocery & Spices
1656 Jane Street
York, ON
(416) 249-3521

Bombay Grocers
1201 Britannia Road West
Mississauga, ON
(905) 813-7091

Bombay Meat Shop
1201 Britannia Road West
(905) 813-7142

Indian Town Food and Spices
641 Markham Road
Scarborough, ON
(416) 438-1013

Indian Supermarket
1053 Dundas West
Mississauga, ON
(905) 848-5420

Malik Grocers
3027 Islington
Toronto, ON
(416) 745-5242

Punjab Supermarket
2652 Islington
Etobicoke, ON
(416) 746-8601

QUEBEC

Apna Bazaar
4852 des Sources
Dollard-des-Ormeaux, PQ
(514) 421-0305

Caravane
1850 St. Catherine West
Montreal, PQ
(514) 935-6656

Epicerie Taaj Oriental
2107 Lapierre
Lasalle, PQ
(514) 363-5784

Marché Bangla Bazar
4705 Van Horne
Montreal, PQ
(514) 738-5363

Marché Victoria Oriental Inc.
4759 des Sources
Pierrefonds, PQ
(514) 685-3280

Marché Priyanka
808 Jean Talon West
Montreal, PQ
(514) 278-5757

Punjab Foods
9000 Bd Newman
Lasalle, PQ
(514) 366-0560

NOVA SCOTIA

Indian Grocery
2585 Robie
Halifax, NS
(902) 423-6639

SASKATCHEWAN

Indian Food Centre
1213 15th Avenue
Regina, SA
(306) 757-9940

ACKNOWLEDGMENTS

Special thanks go to:

Everyone at New Holland Publishing in particular my editor, Clare Sayer, and Rosemary Wilkinson, for all their hard work and for making the idea for the book come to life; Julie Saunders, for typing all the recipes and generally making my very busy life less hectic; the designer, Roger Hammond; John Freeman who, once again, has produced stunning photographs; Sunil Menon for his skill in styling the recipes even when India were playing in the Cricket World Cup!

Everyone at Patak's, in particular those who were involved in the location photography. A special mention goes to the team at Nexus.

And last but not least, thanks to my family and friends without whom I would not have had the inspiration to write this book.

The publishers would also like to thank the following for providing props for the photography:

Abu Sandeep Gallery
55 Beauchamp Place
London SW3 1NY
Tel: 020 7584 7713

Alessi
22 Brook Street
London W1K 5DF
Tel: 020 7518 9091

Cargo Homeshops
Tottenham Court Road
London W1P 7PL
Tel: 020 7580 2895

John Lewis plc
Oxford Street
London W1A 1EX
Tel: 020 7629 7711

Kara Kara
2a Pond Place
London SW3 6QZ
Tel: 020 7591 0891

Muji
Branches nationwide
Tel: 020 7287 7323

Neelam Sarees
388-390 Romford Road
London E7
Tel: 020 8472 2410

The Pier
200 Tottenham Court Road
London W1P 7PL
Tel: 020 7436 9642

Thomas Goode
195 South Audley Street
London W1K 2BN
Tel: 020 7499 2823

The Patak's story

Meena Pathak is the Director of Product Development for the authentic Indian food brand Patak's. Patak's grew from very modest beginnings and is now the number one worldwide Indian food brand – a household name, used by professional chefs and home cooks across the world.

Patak's was founded in the late 1950s by Laxmishanker Pathak, Meena's father-in-law, following his arrival in England with his wife and children. Laxmishanker experienced great difficulty in finding employment and as a means to survive, he began making and selling Indian samosas and snacks from his home. They were well received and soon he had raised sufficient capital to buy his first small shop in North London. The business expanded with the introduction of other authentic Indian products, including pickles and chutneys, and orders flooded in.

Kirit Pathak joined the family business at the age of 17. Meena herself became involved in Patak's shortly after her marriage to Kirit in 1976 when Kirit discovered her creative cooking abilities. Having trained in food technology and hotel management with the prestigious Taj hotel group, Meena had plenty of experience to offer. After a particularly delicious meal she had cooked for the family one evening Kirit asked her, "Can you get that into a jar?", and her career in recipe and product development took off from there.

Throughout the 70s and 80s, the business prospered under Kirit and Meena's guidance. The product portfolio was extended to include pappadums and other Indian accompaniments and, in addition to supplying the Indian restaurant trade with pastes and chutneys, Patak's began exporting its range across the world into mainstream grocery markets.

Meena believes that the key to a successful Indian dish is not just the distinctiveness of the recipe but also the quality and freshness of the

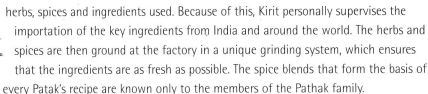

herbs, spices and ingredients used. Because of this, Kirit personally supervises the importation of the key ingredients from India and around the world. The herbs and spices are then ground at the factory in a unique grinding system, which ensures that the ingredients are as fresh as possible. The spice blends that form the basis of every Patak's recipe are known only to the members of the Pathak family.

The company's range has extended over the years from pickles and chutneys, to pastes and cooking sauces in jars and cans, ready-made meals, pappadums, Indian breads and now includes Indian snacks and frozen and chilled meals.

Patak's products are now widely available, enabling consumers to produce their favourite Indian meals at home.

For more information on the company, visit the web site at www.pataks.co.uk.